W9-BRW-034

University of Warwick

Writing the Doctoral Dissertation

A SYSTEMATIC APPROACH

SECOND EDITION

By

GORDON B. DAVIS
Honeywell Professor of Management Information Systems
Carlson School of Management
University of Minnesota

CLYDE A. PARKER
Professor Emeritus, Educational Psychology
University of Minnesota

BARRON'S

All inquiries should be addressed to:

Barron's Educational Series, Inc.
250 Wireless Boulevard
Hauppauge, New York 11788

Library of Congress Catalog Card No. 97-11497
International Standard Book No. 0-8120-9800-5

Library of Congress Cataloging in Publication Data

Davis, Gordon Bitter.
    Writing the doctoral dissertation : a systematic approach / Gordon
B. Davis, Clyde A. Parker. — 2nd ed.
        p.   cm.
    Includes bibliographical references (p.).
    ISBN 0-8120-9800-5
    1. Report writing. 2. Dissertations, Academic. I. Parker, Clyde
Alvin. II. Title.
LB2369.D357   1997
808' .042—dc21   97-11497
                                                              CIP

PRINTED IN THE UNITED STATES OF AMERICA
9 8 7 6 5 4

Contents

Illustrations

Preface

The purpose of this book is to assist doctoral candidates in *completing* a better quality dissertation in a shorter time. Experiences in advising doctoral candidates, in serving on dissertation committees, and in having discussions with candidates as they have worked on their dissertations clearly indicate a need for such a book. The approach is also applicable to master's theses, which can be viewed as limited scope dissertations.

This systematic approach assists doctoral candidates in managing the completion of the dissertation task. It also has advantages for the advisor because the method can improve utilization of scarce faculty resources.

The examples in the text reflect a broad set of experiences, but do not attempt to relate to all conditions that students in different fields may face. One might have considerable discussion about the "truth" or appropriateness of the examples or the format of the forms. This would miss the essence. The examples and forms are used to convey, as concretely as possible, the elements of the approach. The essential point is to structure the dissertation project and to manage it to a successful completion. Students and advisors should feel free to modify the approach to reflect advising style and unique subject area and institutional requirements.

This book was begun while Gordon Davis was on leave from the University of Minnesota as a professor of Management at the European Institute for Advanced Studies in Management, Brussels, Belgium. The work of the Institute involved advising a large number of doctoral candidates in the dissertation stage.

This experience solidified and improved prior ideas and provided an impetus for the text. The faculty of the Institute reviewed parts of the book and made valuable suggestions that are reflected in the final result. The approach has been presented to doctoral candidates in a number of disciplines at the University of Minnesota and several other universities in the United States. It has also been used by doctoral candidates in countries such as Great Britain, Sweden, Belgium, Germany, and France. The response has been very positive, and the results achieved by candidates as they follow the approach have provided ample evidence of its usefulness.

The second edition reflects additional experience with the approach. The basic method remains largely unchanged, although there is added emphasis on identifying the theory or concepts supporting a research topic. Additional background materials include a discussion of the dissertation as knowledge work, the difference between an "entry-level" doctoral and a "midcareer" dissertation, the role of the dissertation in a plan for a scholarly career, and alternative views of methodology. There are changes in the appendices. The three appendices on tools for researching the literature, selected references on research, and using the computer to process analyses were dropped. They quickly became out of date, and more up-to-date references related to a student's academic field should be available. Manuals and other guides to using computer software for analysis of research data are readily available and often part of course work on statistical analysis. A more universal problem for a doctoral student beginning dissertation work is effective use of computer software to improve productivity. A new appendix has been added that addresses this productivity issue.

Comments on the effectiveness of the method and suggestions for improvements in the approach are welcome.

CHAPTER **1**

The Need for a Different Approach to the Dissertation

The student taking courses generally operates on a rather short and well-structured time cycle. Assignments are due each class period, papers are due at a fixed time during the term, and examinations are taken at scheduled times during the term. Research and writing assignments are quite small in scope because they must fit into the framework of a 10-week quarter or a 15-week semester. Even fairly large papers are quite well defined in terms of what needs to be done. The period of doctoral dissertation activities is the first time students have been faced with a large, unstructured project, and usually nothing in their prior training has prepared them for managing such a project. This chapter compares the consequences of a traditional, unstructured approach with those from a structured approach. An understanding of these consequences should provide a doctoral candidate with motivation to follow the systematic approach. Although smaller in scope, the master's thesis is a sufficiently large project so that the same problems of noncompletion occur with dismaying frequency. Therefore, master's candidates can apply the case studies to their situation.

Two Case Studies

The following case studies reflect the activities of real students and illustrate two extremes. One illustrates the consequences of an unmanaged approach; the other, the advantages of a systematic management approach.

JAMES CARTHLY

James Carthly was a fairly good student. He completed his course work with satisfactory grades and passed the qualifying examinations of the doctoral program. After some time, he selected a dissertation topic area in which he had an interest and began collecting data by an interview method. At the same time, during the early spring, he interviewed to take a position with a university. He seemed to be making progress in terms of the background and reading, early data collection, and analysis necessary before one can begin to write the dissertation itself. However, he had never prepared a complete dissertation proposal or a plan for completion. His committee was more or less unaware of the scope of the intended dissertation. They had only a general idea based on his oral comments. There were no meetings of the full committee to discuss the dissertation project. Time passed quickly, and when it was the time for him to begin work at the university where he had accepted a position, there was still no comprehensive proposal or outline of the dissertation for the committee. This didn't worry Carthly because he knew that he had been able to work on the dissertation while doing some teaching as a graduate assistant; he thought there would be even more time for dissertation work with the new position because his teaching load would not be too demanding.

However, he did not anticipate the change in status that came with his new position. He was no longer a graduate student but a young professor (without the thesis completed but, nevertheless, a professor). He now had to teach courses that he had not taught before, so there was much preparation. There were committee meetings to attend, students to advise, and university functions in which to participate. There was a new home to buy, move into, and care for. There were new elementary schools to become acquainted with and a new community to learn about. When Carthly had been a graduate student, living in a graduate student community, there was general agreement between students and spouses that they would forego many normal social functions in order to work the long hours to complete the degrees. The nonstudent spouses often handled many family responsibilities that would normally be shared. Now, he was in a different environment where he was expected to share family responsibilities and have a normal social life.

The day that he passed the qualifying examinations, there had been general rejoicing because now he was almost through. All he had to do was write the "big" paper. Neither he nor his wife was prepared for the scope of the disseration work and the difficulty of completing it. He contributed to this general situation by having no understanding of how long it would take to finish, no plan, and no time schedule. If the subject were broached, he would say, "Well, I'm making good progress. All I have to do is write it up." But months went on with no visible progress on the dissertation.

At the end of the second year, the Dean told Carthly there would be no salary increase because he had not completed the dissertation. No promotion was possible. He began to feel the pressures for completion. He began to work nights and insist that he could not use holidays and vacations for family activities; he must work on the dissertation. After dinner, he would pull out the dissertation and start work. On those nights that he was able to work, he had about four hours. But by the time he got the material arranged, got himself in the proper frame of mind, reviewed what could be done, and brought himself to the point where he could begin work, the actual effective time spent was very low. He was tired and his mind was not alert.

Finally he decided to take part of the summer and return to work at his university, where he could be near his dissertation advisor. The time he spent there, however, was not highly productive. There was no plan or structure that the advisor and he could agree on. The advisor found it difficult to give good guidance. The committee was not called together because there was not sufficient basis for discussion. But they agreed on some general guidelines for the dissertation and on its general scope. The advisor waited for the student to approach him with questions; the student waited for the advisor to contact him. Little was accomplished.

Returning home, Carthly kept working, but progress was slow. The dissertation continued to put a strain on family relations. He always felt that he should be working on the dissertation. His wife felt uncomfortable when they took time for social events or holidays because she had the uneasy feeling that he should be at work. There were no salary raises. He received only temporary appointments. If there had been a cutback, he would have been the first to go. In conferences, Carthly solemnly assured his Dean that work on the dissertation was progressing, and that it should be completed in the coming year. He made these same assurances three years in a row.

Finally, Carthly received notice from his doctoral university that the five-year limit for completion of the dissertation was about to expire. If he did not complete the dissertation within the coming year, he would be terminated as a doctoral student and would not be allowed to complete a doctoral degree. He made arrangements to work full-time on the dissertation during the coming summer, foregoing all income possibilities. The dissertation advisor estimated that Carthly would also need the entire fall semester as well. Therefore, Carthly arranged to leave his family at home, went alone to the university town, and worked full-time on the thesis. He had to ask for an extension on the time limit from the university. Because he was almost through, they were willing to grant the short extension required. He did less for the dissertation than he had originally intended, but he finally completed it.

TED MAREN

Ted Maren had an intuitive feel for how to manage a doctoral dissertation. He selected the general area of his dissertation quite early and structured much of his course work to provide support for it. The papers he wrote for these courses were, in reality, background investigations for the dissertation. He was able to make contacts with professors who were interested in the area that he intended to research. He was able to discuss research methodology and ideas for research with the professors. Much of his course work was related to the dissertation. In the research methodology course, he planned his research design specifically. In a psychology course, he did a paper related to a particular aspect of his research problem. Even though he had not decided upon the exact topic, he knew the general area and was able to work effectively at getting background information, developing a research design, and testing ideas for a possible specific topic.

After passing the qualifying examination, a dissertation committee was appointed. The committee consisted of professors who knew him and were interested in the general area of the proposed dissertation. Maren proceeded to refine the dissertation proposal until the document clearly defined how he intended to conduct the research and the contribution to be made by the dissertation. The committee encouraged him as he developed and sharpened the proposal because they could see the progress he was making. The final proposal, clear and concise, was approved. Maren prepared a time schedule he felt was realistic and followed it as closely as possible. Not everything went as planned. There were some unexpected delays, but he was able to estimate quite closely the actual time of completion. The dissertation was completed approximately two months later than originally planned, but well within the margin of error that he had allowed.

He did excellent work, and at the dissertation defense, it was clear that the dissertation would be accepted. The committee was very familiar with it. They had all participated actively in the supervision. Faculty at the dissertation defense who had not been part of the committee had no difficulty understanding the dissertation or its contribution.

At the university where he accepted employment, Maren was able to begin work immediately in his full professorial role. He began immediately serving on committees and participating in professional activities. There was no need to decline social activities with the excuse that "I have to work on my dissertation." There was no delay in publishing professional articles and doing additional research. He was able to accumulate the necessary publication and research record to justify promotion on a timely basis. He had learned to enjoy scholarly work, and it was evident that he was well on his way to a productive career.

The Consequences of Delay in Completion

The most serious possible consequence of a delay in completion is that the doctoral dissertation will never be written and the doctorate will never be obtained. Completion of the dissertation is the big hurdle in obtaining the doctorate. Perhaps as many as one-third of doctoral candidates complete the course requirements, but never the dissertation.

The effects of delay in completion are serious even if there is eventual completion. As a consequence of the delay, the candidate's original committee, perhaps even the advisor, may no longer be available. The topic may no longer be timely. Others may have done research that goes beyond or replaces what he or she is doing. An academic or other career is made much less rewarding. Promotion is made difficult or impossible. There are lost opportunities for writing and other research. The constant pressure to work on the dissertation and complete it disturbs the candidate's personal life and reduces effectiveness at work. The dissertation was intended to be a demonstration of ability to do research—the first step in a productive research career. Instead, it has discouraged further research because the project was not completed on a timely basis. If the candidate finally does turn in a completed dissertation that is accepted, he or she is likely to have little enthusiasm for doing more individual research.

The Advantages of Planning and Careful Management

The advantages of timely, planned completion may be inferred from the disadvantages of delayed completion. It is possible to expect improved professional opportunities, improved dissertation quality, and greatly increased incentive to further research. In addition, advantages commonly occur related to financial aid.

Students usually need to apply well in advance for financial aid for support of dissertation work. Applications require that the student present a dissertation proposal along with the application. Many students without a completion plan do not have a good proposal and, therefore, are unable to apply for the aid. Students seem willing to borrow money and seek other financial aid for the period when they are taking courses, but seem quite reluctant to take financial risks at the dissertation stage. From a logical standpoint, borrowing is most appropriate for the completion of the dissertation. Everyone who has had to delay completion of the dissertation can attest to the fact that it reduced income, with the effect lasting even beyond the final completion. This suggests that timely completion commonly has a positive financial payoff. A student who is considering borrowing money might well hesitate if there is uncertainty about the dissertation process and sufficient progress has not been made. However, a student who is following a plan for doing the dissertation, has a reasonable time schedule, and has an accepted proposal can be reasonably confident that the project will be completed on time. He or she can therefore take the financial risks necessary to complete the dissertation.

The Problem of the First Position

Many students think a dissertation is just a "big paper," and they think they can do it without too much difficulty. They underestimate the time required and take a position before they are finished. Recruiting for academic positions is commonly done early in the year. Some students make the commitment for September during the preceding winter. The student who has begun work on a dissertation in January may feel it will be completed by September. However, unless there has been good planning and scheduling of the work, this is likely to be a false hope.

The first step in solving this problem is for the student to follow a systematic plan and establish a firm completion date. The second step is to negotiate a delayed entry into the first position if the dissertation is not completed. When there was faculty shortage, many schools encouraged prospective faculty members to come without completing the dissertation. Commonly, the result was a faculty with many long-standing members who never completed their doctoral dissertations. Many schools now have pressures to increase their percentage of professors with doctorates. Therefore, schools are interested in the candidate with a completed doctorate.

The student should discuss frankly with a prospective employer the commitment to complete the doctorate before leaving the university. Completion means an approved draft. The final editing, publication, and other requirements, such as the final dissertation defense, can take place after the student is settled in the new position. But even these steps are better handled before the student leaves. If the student raises the subject and expresses a commitment to finish, it is likely that the university or other employer with whom the student is negotiating will agree to a delayed arrival (at the second semester, for example) if there is an inability to complete the dissertation. Generalizations cannot apply to all employers, but based on the experiences of doctoral candidates who have followed this advice, there is an increasing willingness by universities to agree to these conditions. Such negotiation is more likely to be successful if the student is following a systematic plan for completing the dissertation, with a schedule of activities and a realistic time estimate for completion. The only way a student can make reasonably valid statements as to when the dissertation will be finished is by having such a plan. Casual, intuitive projections almost always underestimate the time required for completion.

The Philosophy of the Systematic Approach

Three propositions underlie the recommendations in the systematic approach to completing a doctoral dissertation.

1. Structuring of the dissertation project can significantly improve performance (by means of topic analyses, proposal documents, plans, schedules, and so on, described in the systematic approach).
2. The student has primary responsibility for the management of the doctoral dissertation project.
3. Faculty (advisor and committee) are a scarce resource.

The first proposition implies that the productivity gap between managed and unmanaged doctoral dissertation work is large. The same theme in a larger context was stated by a well-regarded researcher in management:

> To make knowledge work productive will be the great management task of this century just as to make manual work productive was the great management task of the last century. The gap between knowledge work that is left unmanaged is probably a great deal wider than was the tremendous difference between manual work before and after the introduction of scientific management. [Peter Drucker, *The Age of Discontinuity* (New York: Harper and Row, 1969), page 272.]

The doctoral dissertation is a large undertaking with certain risks regarding completion and acceptance. However, the risk can be substantially reduced and the probabilities of successful and timely completion can be greatly improved by following a systematic approach to the management of the dissertation project. The objective of the approach is to *complete* a good doctoral dissertation in a reasonable time, but there are some other benefits for students successfully following the approach. Students may gain confidence in their ability to structure and manage research. They will probably do better research following the dissertation. As successful candidates become faculty advisors, an improved understanding of research and dissertation management will probably result, and they will become better advisors.

The second proposition places responsibility for dissertation management on the student. This proposition is reasonable because the dissertation is *the* evidence that the doctoral candidate is capable of independently making a contribution to a field of knowledge. Unfortunately, many students are not able to manage the venture well. In many cases, the doctoral dissertation is the first large, unstructured project undertaken by a graduate student. The student may have worked closely with the advisor or other faculty members on significant research projects; indeed, in some cases the doctoral research is an extension of such cooperative research. More often, however, the student has not had such experience and is working alone in a nebulous and ambiguous venture. The advisor and committee provide much help, but it is the student's project; the student must take the responsibility for initiation, planning, executing, and writing.

The third proposition recognizes that faculty advisors are a scarce but important resource for the dissertation project. The advisor serves as a sponsor, a guide, a critic, a facilitator, and an important source of support. If the advisor performs this role well, the frustrations that the student encounters are minimized. Some advisors are better able to facilitate the completion of students' dissertations than others. The exact nature and cause of these advisor differences vary; the student should recognize that they exist.

The systematic approach assumes a mutual understanding of advisor-student roles. There is a personal, implied contract between the student and the advisor that the advisor will

* provide guidance;
* respond to the papers given to read within a reasonable time;
* be reasonably consistent in advice;
* protect the student from unreasonable demands;
* assist the student at those times when the voice of a faculty member advocate is necessary;
* generally aid the student in pursuing the dissertation project.

In this relationship, the student doing the dissertation is expected to

* do what he or she says will be done when promised (or explain why it cannot be done);
* have integrity in research and writing;
* keep in communication;
* prepare documents for comment;
* follow a method of presentation that effectively uses the advisor's and committee's time;
* be reasonable in making demands on the time of the advisor and the committee;
* be open to suggestions and to advice, but also show initiative.

Advisors have different advising styles. What is appropriate for one might not be quite right for another. However, this dissertation management approach should be useful to all advisors. It should improve the relationship between the student and the advisor and help to raise the quality of the dissertation. Also, the procedures outlined in the text will help minimize problems in advising and maximize the probabilities of success. The techniques provide for documentation of the dissertation project. This is especially helpful when changes in the advisor or committee occur.

Students may use the approach unwisely, but generally it appears to have advantages for both the advisor and the student.

An experienced advisor knows all of the suggestions in the approach. The value of the publication is that it codifies the advice in a single, short manual. Therefore, the new advisor may also find this manual helpful in becoming a good advisor.

The text has been written so that a candidate may take the initiative in deciding to follow the method or an advisor may ask a student to obtain the manual and use the approach. In either case, the advisor may wish to specify amendments or differences in style for the student to follow. For example, one advisor may find it expedient to have the student prepare an agenda for all committee meetings and to distribute it to the committee members after the advisor approves it. Another faculty member may feel that an agenda is something the advisor should do alone and, therefore, may tell the student that the agenda suggested in the management approach should not be followed.

Limitations

This short book is normative. It presents a management process for *completing* a quality doctoral dissertation in a reasonable time. The danger of a normative presentation is that the process appears mechanical—just follow the steps and the dissertation is done. In reality, the process never works exactly as described. There is backtracking and numerous iterations. There are failures and restarts. These are not justification for a lack of management. Lack of management in the dissertation process will most certainly result in a higher rate of wasted effort and higher probability of not finishing. The dangers from applying too much structure to the management of the dissertation are much less than the consequences of too little.

The process emphasizes management and discipline; it speaks little to creativity and passion for research. Students who do best have reasonable creativity and passion for their research. These are vital elements. They are not emphasized because they are assumed to exist. The issue for this text is how to channel the creativity and passion into a disciplined process that results in a quality dissertation in a reasonable time.

The text in its descriptions and examples tends to emphasize traditional positivist, hypothesis testing research, but this reflects the dominant research paradigm, rather than a prescription. The management approach is equally effective with interpretive research. In fact, good management of the process may be more important in research methods that have less natural closure.

Summary

The problem is that students either don't complete the doctoral dissertation or take an unduly long time to do it. Many factors compound the problem, such as the need for financial support and the need to make an advance commitment for a position. However, much of the difficulty can be traced to students not knowing how to manage a dissertation project. Nothing in their prior experience has adequately prepared them for it. As a result, they misallocate their efforts, delay in structuring the project, and make unrealistic time estimates. These problems prompted the approach described in this manual.

2

An Overview of the Dissertation Management Approach

Students write a doctoral dissertation because it is required for a doctor of philosophy (Ph.D.) degree and also for closely related doctorates in education and other similar fields.[1] Periodically, there are suggestions that a different doctorate be given to those candidates who intend only to be teachers and that the dissertation should not be required for students who do not intend to do research. These suggestions have so far not received significant support. The students themselves sense that such a doctorate, without a doctoral dissertation, would be viewed by their colleagues as a lesser degree. The doctoral dissertation was instituted as a requirement for good reasons. The reasons are more applicable to some students than for others. However, as long as the requirement exists, students should plan to do it well and make the dissertation project beneficial to their careers. While the systematic approach is written in terms of the doctoral dissertation, it requires only a slight shift in emphasis to make it directly applicable to the master's thesis.

---

[1] A few fields—such as dentistry, medicine, and law—use the term *doctor* in their degrees, but there is no research or thesis requirement comparable to that of the Ph.D.

The Objectives of a Doctoral Dissertation

Although there may be variations in the way different academic programs view the doctoral dissertation, the requirement appears generally aimed at achieving three objectives having to do with demonstrating the competence of the candidate to

1. do independent research;
2. make a contribution to knowledge with the research;
3. document the research and make it available to the scholarly community (I.E., write the dissertation).

The dissertation is both a documentation that the candidate has done independent research and that there is a contribution to knowledge. From the standpoint of the university, there is no demonstrated ability and no contribution from the research unless the dissertation document is written.

The Nature of the Dissertation Task

What is a doctoral dissertation? It is the documentation of independent research that makes a contribution to knowledge. It is not just a "paper" that is bigger than the ones students have written in connection with various courses. The factors of size, independent research, and contribution place the dissertation in a class apart from prior papers.

The median page length for a dissertation is about 225 pages, but page lengths range from under 100 pages to over 600 pages (Figure 2-1). There are some length differences among academic disciplines, but these differences are not significant. Doctoral students may wish to analyze the length of recent dissertations in their field as a rough indicator of expectations. The distribution will generally fit a log-normal distribution—that is, the mean is larger than the median because long dissertations are not offset by short dissertations (Figure 2-2). There is a natural lower limit, but not a corresponding upper limit.

Using a reasonable estimate for median length of 225 pages, a mean of 240 pages, and a log-normal distribution, a rough idea

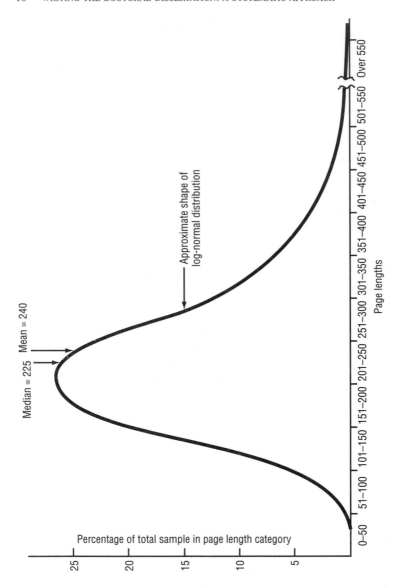

2-1. Estimated length distribution of pages for doctoral dissertations in social sciences and humanities.

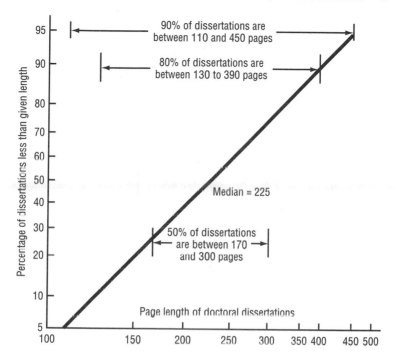

2-2. Estimated page lengths of doctoral dissertations plotted as log-normal cumulative distribution.

of the distribution of lengths can be inferred. We estimate that:

- 50 percent of dissertations are from 170 to 300 pages;
- 80 percent of dissertations are from 130 to 390 pages;
- 90 percent of dissertations are from 110 to 450 pages.

It is more difficult to estimate time spent on dissertations. Using a log-normal distribution, we estimate that actual, effective time (actual working hours) for doing a doctoral dissertation from start to finish is about 15 175-hour work months (2,625 hours). Based on distribution in Figure 2-3, we estimate

- 50 percent of dissertations take from 13½ to 18 work months;
- 80 percent of dissertations require 12 to 20 work months;

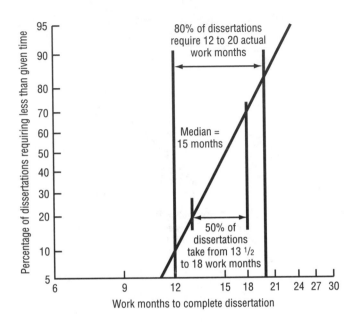

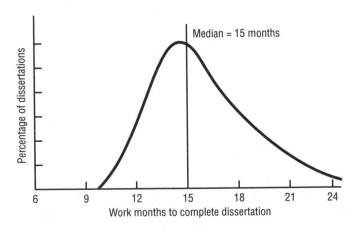

2-3. Estimated actual work months from start of topic search to completed draft of doctoral dissertation (author's estimates).

- 5 percent of dissertations require 11 or less work months;
- 5 percent of dissertations require 22 or more work months.

It should be noted that, unlike the page estimates, which are based on an analysis of actual dissertation page lengths, the estimates in Figure 2-3 are rough estimates based on observations of student performance. There appear to be differences in time spent on dissertations related to the field of study, but these are not well documented.

Given the uncertainties of a dissertation project, what is the value of the page and time estimates? They set expectations and assist in planning. A student who plans a 1,000-page dissertation will find that it takes substantially more time. The student may still choose to do the project, but it will be with the knowledge that the length is four times the median length. The time estimates lack data for validating them, but they appear reasonable. Again, they assist in setting expectations and limits on the scope of a dissertation. If a student has expectations that a typical dissertation will take 15 *effective* work months, these expectations can be used in deciding the scope of work to be included in the dissertation. Work not included in the dissertation may still be part of a student's research plan, but it can be delayed until after the dissertation.

The time estimates represent actual, effective work hours devoted, not the elapsed time during which the candidate worked on the project. The elapsed time over which the work is performed is generally one-and-a-half to three years. Many students take five or more years to complete the dissertation. Some universities have a rule that dissertations must be completed within a certain time (for example, five years) after the qualifying examination has been passed. But other universities establish no cutoff, and students still claim to be working on dissertations ten or more years after they have completed all work but the dissertation.

The size of the dissertation makes it substantially different from any paper the student has ever done. It is also unstructured.

Up to the point of the dissertation, the student has performed academically in a highly structured environment. Professors who formerly told the student what to do and how to do it now act as if the student knows what to do. They say, "It's your dissertation. What do you want to do? How do you want to approach the problem? What methodology are you going to use?"

A key element in the dissertation is the contribution the dissertation makes. It is difficult to express what is meant by contribution to knowledge. However, the concept is explored in more detail in Chapter 6.

The question of how good a dissertation should be is difficult to answer. There are students who never complete the dissertation because they view it as requiring such high quality that they don't believe they can achieve that quality. The student should probably take a reasonable attitude toward the quality of the doctoral dissertation. One should do a good job as a beginning step in a career, but should not view it as his or her magnum opus. It is unlikely that a dissertation will be the highlight of a student's career because it is usually done at the beginning of the scholarly career, not at the height. There are a few examples of scholars who have made their major contribution with their doctoral dissertation, but this is not normally so.

In summary, the dissertation task is to carry out a research project that contributes to knowledge and to document the project and its contribution in a written document. The scope of the project can vary, but a typical doctoral dissertation project will require 15 work months, and the documentation will average a length of 225 pages.

The Life Cycle of a Dissertation Project

The dissertation project represents a process of reducing uncertainty. The student begins with the notion of doing research in a broad area of investigation in which there might be thousands of dissertation possibilities. The student must reduce the uncertainty by reducing the number of possibilities he or she is going to consider. This is done by looking closely at several topics and evaluating each. One of the topics is selected and then further defined by the dissertation proposal. Uncertainty is again reduced when a detailed chapter outline is prepared. Uncertainty is eliminated when the research has been done, the text of the dissertation has been written, and the committee has approved it.

The process does not always move as smoothly as explained. The student may look at several topics, select one, do some investigation, but find that the topic will not work out. The candidate selects another topic and develops a new proposal. The proposal, when first presented, has many uncertainties and ambiguities. By working with the committee, the proposal is finally made sharper and more definite until finally the exact task to be performed has been defined. The life cycle of a dissertation can thus be thought of as going from the general to the specific. The events that mark the reduction in generality until a dissertation is finally accepted are as follows:

1. Selection of general area for research
2. Selection of several topics for evaluation
3. Selection and exploration of one topic and completion of dissertation proposal
4. Completion of detailed chapter outlines
5. Completion of literature search
6. Completion of research and analysis
7. Completion of text of dissertation
8. Acceptance by committee

The systematic management plan described in the text will illustrate how to proceed through these general steps, how to use various methods to focus on a particular problem, and how to obtain assistance from a dissertation committee and an advisor.

Figure 2-4 provides a general idea of how the time for a dissertation is spent. The time may vary considerably from these rough estimates. Between 25 and 30 percent of the total hours will be occupied with writing the dissertation drafts, revising them, proofreading and correcting them, and revising them again. It comes as a surprise to many candidates that the actual writing occupies so much time. This will receive further explanation in Chapter 7.

Work Months		Percentage
5	Writing, editing, and proofing	33%
7	Research and analysis	47%
1	Complete search of prior research	7%
2	Topic adjustment and proposal	13%
15		100%

2-4. Allocation of effort in a typical doctoral dissertation.

The Overall Management Approach

The management approach described in this text has the following three major elements:
1. Predissertation stage activities
2. Selection of the dissertation topic
3. Management of research and writing

Each of these will be explained in detail in later chapters; the content of the three elements will be surveyed here. A checklist of major activities associated with the approach is found on the inside back cover.

PREDISSERTATION STAGE ACTIVITIES

If possible, the student should begin to think of the dissertation well before reaching dissertation stage. Ideally, the dissertation will initiate a line of research that can then be followed for some years. The choice should influence the planning of doctoral courses and especially the courses taken outside of the major field, such as research methodology and minor fields or supporting programs. The early selection of a research area will allow the candidate to obtain desirable background, do predissertation investigation as part of course work requirements, and develop committee contacts among professors who have an interest in the area. A student should begin, as soon as possible, to compile a dissertation topic file for cogent ideas, together with all the supporting evidence that is available at the time.

SELECTION OF THE DISSERTATION TOPIC

In some cases, the dissertation topic is "assigned" by an advisor. In most instances, the selection of the dissertation topic is an iterative activity involving both student and faculty members. Rarely does a student have a well-defined topic in the beginning. Generally, the initial topic is poorly defined, too general, and too large in scope. It usually requires several iterations before the topic is refined and a good dissertation proposal is developed. The systematic management approach begins by examining several possibilities, putting these into a topic analysis format, consulting with the advisor and dissertation committee, and selecting one of the topics to pursue in more detail. The selected topic is expanded into a dissertation proposal. The initial proposal is clarified, expanded, reduced, and refined, until it is sufficiently explicit so that the committee can agree it is an acceptable project of the scope and quality suitable for a doctoral dissertation.

MANAGEMENT OF RESEARCH AND WRITING

Every student working on a dissertation should draw up a schedule for completion. The plan should show the candidate how much time is available and provide a good idea of the amount of time that can be spent on each of the various activities required for the dissertation. The candidate should use various methods for improving the working relationship with the advisor and the committee. These include written documents, summaries of meetings and discussions, issue summaries and chapter outlines for chapters, and agendas for meetings. These activities generally help make the relationship between the advisor and the committee more productive. The candidate should actively plan and control the dissertation activities. A few hours each month spent in planning and control will generally increase the productivity of the work time.

3

The Dissertation as Knowledge Work

In Chapter 1, the point was made that doing research and writing a dissertation is a prime example of "knowledge work," and knowledge work that is managed will be more productive. This is such an essential point that this chapter will provide concepts and principles for improving productivity in knowledge work.[1] These concepts and principles apply directly to the doctoral dissertation; they are also applicable to the work that graduates of doctoral programs will do in their careers.

Knowledge work is contrasted with manual work and clerical work. The principles for getting the work done and achieving high productivity differ for these three types of work. While productivity can apply to both individuals and teams or groups, the discussion will focus on individual productivity because a dissertation is an individual effort. The principles and methods for individual productivity in knowledge work are generally simple and intuitive. However, they are often ignored.

Two other important issues affecting the nature of the dissertation as knowledge work are the position of the dissertation in a career and the role of the dissertation in a career plan. Preparation for doing a doctoral dissertation is generally defined by each doctoral program. This preparation is affected by different views about the place of the dissertation in a scholarly career, whether it is primarily at the beginning of a scholarly career or

---

[1]Based on Gordon B. Davis and J. David Naumann, *Personal Productivity with Information Technology* (New York: McGraw-Hill Book Co., 1997).

in mid-career. The implications of these two views will be explained as background for dissertation work. The dissertation is a noteworthy accomplishment. For those who pursue a scholarly career, it is a significant milestone. Positioning the dissertation in a scholarly career will aid in making decisions about the topic of the dissertation and methodology to be employed. The chapter will survey the place of a dissertation in career planning.

Definition of Knowledge Work

A general definition of *knowledge work* is human mental work performed to generate useful information. In doing it, knowledge workers access data, use knowledge, employ mental models, and apply significant concentration and attention.[2] Examples of knowledge workers include professors, writers, financial analysts, system analysts, managers, accountants, lawyers, and so forth. Although there are exceptions, knowledge workers tend to be in professional positions requiring university education. The positions require creative, innovative, and problem-solving skills.

Knowledge workers are valued for their knowledge and expertise. Based on education and experience, they are expected to have personal knowledge and skill to perform the activities of knowledge work. They are expected to have knowledge of the domain (such as law, medicine, accounting) in which they work plus the processes and procedures for performing its knowledge work. Although an organization may provide some procedures for knowledge workers to follow, they are expected to be able to apply generally accepted procedures and to innovate with processes and procedures appropriate to the specific organization and its situation.

The definition of *knowledge work* is relevant to the work of a doctoral student in doing research and writing a dissertation.

---

[2]Ibid, p.7.

The elements in the definition that describe the type of work, the objective, and four dominant process characteristics can be applied to doctoral dissertation work.

- *The type of work: human mental work.* The mental work involves human information processing. It is cognitive work rather than physical work. The research for a dissertation may involve some clerical work, but the dominant characteristic of a dissertation is mental work.

- *The objective: to generate useful information.* Ideas, analyses, evaluations, instructions, programs, plans, assurances, reasoning, and arguments are examples of useful information. A dissertation adds to knowledge and is useful in expanding the evidence for knowledge.

- *Four dominant process characteristics:* In performing dissertation work, individuals perform processes that access data, access knowledge, employ mental models, and require significant concentration and attention.

    access data. Dissertation work involves acquisition of data, either by direct data capture procedures or by retrieving from stored data. Examples are searching the literature and collecting data for analysis.

    access knowledge. The person doing dissertation work must access knowledge to perform the task. A knowledge worker either has the required knowledge (internal) or knows where and how to find it (external). The course work and projects of a doctoral program plus prior education and experience provide the doctoral student with knowledge necessary to do the dissertation.

    employ mental models. Individuals performing dissertation work employ mental models of the processes to be followed and the outputs to be produced. A set of research propositions and a research model generally underlie the approach to a dissertation.

require significant concentration and attention. The performance of dissertation work is not effortless; it requires mental or cognitive effort and significant concentration and attention. This characteristic makes a dissertation hard work. It is one reason that good management of the dissertation project can reduce the total time and improve the result.

Productivity in Knowledge Work (Like a Dissertation)

Productivity in physical production is measured by the resources required to produce a unit of the product. For example, farming productivity is based on the human labor, capital, fertilizer, and other raw materials used to produce a unit such as a bushel of grain. Traditional productivity measures are inadequate to measure productivity in knowledge work. Are two analyses in a dissertation worth twice as much as one? Is a 20-page chapter worth twice as much as a 10-page chapter? Productivity in knowledge work is reflected in the time and energy that the knowledge worker expends to achieve a result with desired quality.

In performing knowledge work, an individual is limited by time, mental energy, and attention. Time is limited; there are only so many hours available. However, the hours made available for dissertation activity may be affected by motivation. If the work is motivating, the individual may spend additional hours on it; if it's not, the individual may tire more easily and spend less time on it. Mental energy is not fixed in quantity; it can be expanded significantly by motivation or reduced by demotivating events or processes. Attention is an individual cognitive resource; a human has a limited ability to focus on an activity. Attention may be used profitably, or it may be wasted on activities not requiring it.

Productivity in doing a dissertation follows the general principles for knowledge work productivity. There are essentially five ways productivity may be improved in doing a dissertation or other knowledge work:

- Improve motivation
- Improve task management
- Conserve attention
- Reduce errors and omissions
- Eliminate redundant processes

IMPROVE MOTIVATION

Motivation affects all work, whether manual, clerical, or knowledge work. However, the effects on knowledge work tend to be much larger. A manual worker loading a truck with boxes of products will work faster with fewer errors if motivated to do so; likewise, a clerical worker will prepare more customer invoices with fewer errors if highly motivated. A knowledge worker who is highly motivated is able to concentrate more fully on the task and has more mental energy to apply to the work than a poorly motivated worker. The difference in performance from motivation tends to be much larger with knowledge workers than with manual and clerical workers.

High motivation tends to increase individual commitment to high-quality performance. High motivation also tends to energize a person and increase the cognitive resources that are applied to the activities being performed. If bored or unmotivated, a person tends to reduce the attention, concentration, and energy devoted to the task. In other words, increased motivation increases an individual's willingness and ability to perform work. While individual knowledge workers cannot control all sources of motivation, they can increase work motivation with an interesting task, a task design with feedback, and a task design with frequent completions.

Dissertations should be interesting; however, some activities are more interesting than others. It may be possible to divide and structure individual activities to maintain interest. Getting feedback from activities is usually motivating. For example, feedback from a dissertation advisor on progress will usually provide motivation to keep working with enthusiasm.

Individuals tend to be motivated by task completion. In other words, completing a task, however small, provides positive feedback and motivation. This suggests that an individual should break down large tasks into smaller ones, each taking a fairly short period of time (perhaps no more than one week). Each small task has a well-defined deliverable. A dissertation may take 15 work months to complete, but there are numerous subtasks that may take a few days or a few weeks. Defining completion for these subtasks by progress notes, write-ups, reports to advisor, and sections for the dissertation can provide motivation when the subtask is completed.

IMPROVE TASK MANAGEMENT

Motivation and task management are interconnected. Good task management will improve motivation. Three ways to improve task management for dissertation work are task planning, task scheduling, and stopping rules.

Planning of knowledge work tends to be a cognitive bargain. In other words, the time and mental energy devoted to planning a dissertation is more than recovered by improved performance and reduced time and energy spent doing the activities. It reduces wasted time and improves synergy among activities. Planning includes the division of the dissertation task into short subtasks that provide completion motivation.

Scheduling of work is important to productivity because it reduces productivity losses caused by scheduling and improves the use of a knowledge worker's scarce resources of time and energy. Productivity losses caused by scheduling include unproductive waiting time (that might be profitably used for other activities) or schedule delays caused by a failure to begin activities at the proper time. With a dissertation, there are periods of waiting for comments, waiting for research sites to respond, waiting for questionnaires to be returned, and so on. Scheduling activities such as writing or editing chapters, searching literature, and so forth during these waiting periods improves productivity.

Scheduling also improves the utilization of time and energy. Individuals tend to have a daily cycle of energy and alertness. High-value knowledge work activities should therefore be scheduled for times of the day when energy and alertness are highest. Because an individual doing a dissertation has a mixture of difficult cognitive work and relatively simple clerical work (some of it so simple it might be termed *rest work*), scheduling difficult cognitive work at times of highest energy will result in a greater achievement of deliverables and increased motivation from the completion. The dissertation rest work is scheduled during times when motivation is low or during periods of rest following hard cognitive work. In the case of a dissertation, preparing research designs and research instruments, analyzing data, and interpreting results are difficult cognitive activities; editing previously written chapters and writing thank you notes to research participants are cognitively simple activities. Conservation of scarce knowledge work resources is usually most effective when there is explicit scheduling (as opposed to intuitive scheduling without a formal scheduling mechanism). One of the problems with intuitive scheduling is that the schedule may be overly influenced by interruptions and demands for immediate action. Also, it has been observed that activities that are well structured are attractive in an intuitive schedule and are often done first (structured activities drive out unstructured ones).

Stopping rules are decision rules for deciding when to stop working on a project and declare that it is finished. An important characteristic of knowledge work is the absence of a physical basis for stopping work. There are no practical limits on the amount of time that can be spent on a knowledge work task. Manual work and clerical work tend to have both physical limits and time limits; the only strict stopping rule for knowledge work is a deadline. For example, a worker digging a ditch is finished when the ditch has been dug. A clerical worker entering payment data is finished when the transactions have been entered. A knowledge worker doing financial analysis and preparing a report can expand the analysis almost without limit and can redo and rework the report again and again. A student doing dissertation research can keep working indefinitely. It is possible to keep working on more references, more data, more analyses, and more editing. Developing and applying appropriate stopping rules for dissertation activities is therefore an important part of productivity in doing a dissertation. The stopping rules can be based on a planned amount of time, such as time searching for references; improvement from added work, such as improvement in evidence or reasoning from more analysis or more editing; or achievement of satisfactory results. Productive people tend to follow the principle of satisficing, that is, stopping when satisfactory results have been achieved.

CONSERVE ATTENTION

Humans are limited in their ability to pay attention and concentrate on activities. In other words, humans have limited attentional resources. Although high motivation may induce some increase in attentional resources and poor motivation may reduce the availability of attention, there are still limits. A critical limit in knowledge work such as a dissertation is the ability to concentrate attention on activities. Three methods for conserving attention are automatic processing, expertise, and reuse of existing formats and structures.

Attentional resources may be conserved by making activities automatic or substantially automatic. Activities become automatic by being routinized as standard procedures or processes. Repeating established sequences of operations makes them automatic. For example, driving an automobile is substantially automatic for an experienced driver as is executing certain software commands for an experienced user. Some fairly difficult activities can be made automatic by repetition; others are difficult to automate. For example, planning is a significant user of attentional resources because planning has a high level of uncertainty and complexity. Uncertainty is increased because of the number of possible combinations of events that must be considered. Information technology supports automatic processing, both by automating activities with computers and by providing opportunities for automating sequences of activities using computers. In doing dissertation work, for example, a student who becomes expert in proper citation practices can reduce otherwise difficult cognitive work to fairly automatic processing.

Expertise improves use of attentional resources because experts tend to be more selective in activities requiring attention, such as the search and retrieval of information. They focus on the important data and usually have more automatic processing behavior. In doing dissertation work, a student who becomes expert in literature search can be more selective in search activities.

Doing the work to complete a task typically involves both work design and performing the operations in the work design. The design of processes and procedures may take more time than the execution of the operations. For example, formulating the structure of a dissertation chapter (the framework of the chapter and the flow of logic to be developed) may take as much time as the writing. Design resources use attentional resources and require the application of creativity and design logic. Reusing formats, processes, and procedures can significantly improve performance. It can reduce the time and mental effort to design new ones; reduce communication, training, and learning costs; and increase automatic processing. Reusable processes and procedures are a form of memory for both an individual and an organization. The reusable procedure is "recalled" from the memory of an individual or from stored representations, such as forms, procedures manuals, instructions, and computer programs. Reusable procedures can usually result in more use of automatic processing, but they must be learned and used often enough to achieve it. The reuse of procedures is vital to productivity in dissertation work. Selecting and following a standard format for the chapters, figures and tables, citations, references, presentation of data, and so forth reduce the work design time for the dissertation. The earlier these selections are made, the earlier their use will be somewhat automatic.

REDUCE ERRORS AND OMISSIONS

Errors and omissions reduce productivity because error detection and correction take significant resources. For example, to detect and correct an error in a document or an analysis will often take from two to ten times as much time as the original writing or analysis.

Errors and omissions can be reduced by careful work, careful documentation, use of information technology, and expertise. Careful work and documentation often benefits from selection, learning, and repeated use of procedures. In the case of a dissertation, this includes standard methods for recording investigator notes and documenting time, place, person, and so on.

Information technology software assists in recording and retrieving information. Software functions also aid in locating errors in data and in the dissertation text. Statistical software functions are useful in detecting missing data items. Software for storing and analyzing data has functions for detecting incorrect data in a data set. These include range tests to determine if data items are within a specified range, zero and sign tests to detect these conditions if they are incorrect, data type tests to detect data not in correct type format, and test for relationships among data items. Word processors contain search functions to find missing references (citations, tables, figures, and chapters) and to search and replace references that have changed. Spell checkers can detect incorrect spelling and grammar checkers can detect common grammatical mistakes. Use of software is explained further in the Appendix.

Expertise is also important in detecting and correcting errors. Over time, experts develop a mental model that allows errors in data to be detected based on a comparison of the data with a mental model of what the data should be. The expert may also be influenced by the context associated with the data. For example, expert knowledge about the nature of financial institutions may allow a researcher to spot errors in a factor analysis related to them.

ELIMINATE REDUNDANT PROCESSES

Redundancy is defined as the existence of operations and data that are unnecessary because they duplicate other operations or stored data. For example, an individual performing analysis on organization data may re-enter the data. This is a redundant operation because the data already exist in the data storage of the organization. Insofar as possible, redundancy should be eliminated, unless there is some operational or control reason for it.

In dissertation work, redundant processes are often caused by failure to plan ahead for the data needed. For example, an incomplete reference will require a repeat of the search, failure to get data from an informant may require a second interview, and failure to request an analysis will require additional processing. Computer software provides functions to reduce redundant processes. For example, a spreadsheet with a complex analysis may be included in a dissertation appendix but certain key parts of the spreadsheet may be incorporated in a dissertation chapter. To rekey the data from the spreadsheet is redundant because it is possible to copy the parts needed and paste them into the chapter. If the spreadsheet may change during analysis, the spreadsheet may be linked to the chapter, so that any change in the spreadsheet is automatically made in the text. These functions to eliminate redundant processes also reduce errors and omissions in re-entering data. As a second example, a dissertation will need a table of contents with the chapter titles, major headings, and minor headings along with page numbers. A typical feature of a word processing software package is a function to mark each title, heading, and subheading for the table of contents. When it is time to produce the table of contents, executing a simple table of contents function will retrieve all entries with page numbers without error and without additional entry of items.

Redundant operations are also caused by a failure to adopt a standard format for chapters, figures, tables, and references. This failure leads to redundant work in that it requires the individual to reformat the elements and place them in a consistent form.

Position of Dissertation in a Scholarly Career

The basic concept of a doctoral dissertation as a contribution to knowledge is essentially the same for all universities in all countries. However, there are differences in the structure of doctoral programs and the acceptance process for a dissertation. They can be traced, to a great extent, to the position of a doctoral dissertation in a scholarly career. Other differences reflect history and custom. The two positions of a doctoral dissertation in a scholarly career are entry-level doctorate and midcareer doctorate.

- An entry-level doctorate assumes the candidate has had very little experience as a scholar and researcher. Therefore, the doctoral program includes course work, research experiences with a faculty mentor or under close faculty supervision, and a dissertation that is supervised by a committee of faculty members with the advisor as one member. This model is dominant in North America.

• A midcareer doctorate assumes that the candidate is engaged in a scholarly career, is teaching, has written some papers, and is now ready to do a dissertation as a demonstration of scholarly maturity and performance. A single dissertation advisor is appointed to supervise the dissertation. This model has been used in many European countries.

The implications of these differences are reflected in the amount of structure imposed on a doctoral program, the checkpoints imposed on progress, and so forth. One critical difference is the final approval process.

• In an entry-level doctoral program, the dissertation has typically been tracked by a committee with the advisor as a key member. The committee has probably either formally or informally, reviewed the dissertation research proposal and indicated approval of the question and the proposed research methods to be applied. This same committee gives the final approval on the dissertation. The final defense is a quality control procedure, but if the candidate has been in residence and kept in touch with his or her dissertation committee, most issues will have been resolved before the public, final oral.

• In a midcareer doctoral program, the use of a single advisor leads to strong review processes with independent experts. External reviewers are appointed who have had no prior interaction relative to the dissertation. The external examiners' reading is followed by a final defense that may include spirited discussion of the merits of the case for and against acceptance.

The general trend worldwide is toward a requirement that scholars have the doctorate before beginning a scholarly career. The trend has been accompanied by changes in many midcareer programs to an entry-level doctorate model. Although this discussion of the two models is simplified and other factors are also important, it helps explain differences in the way students in different countries approach the dissertation process. The systematic method described in this book is oriented to the advisor plus committee structure associated with an entry-level doctorate; however, the basic concepts can be equally useful for a person working under a midcareer model.

The Dissertation in a Plan for a Scholarly Career

Commonly, doctoral students view the dissertation as one more hurdle in getting a doctorate. For those not planning a scholarly career, this view makes some sense. For those doing a doctorate at entry into a scholarly career, the dissertation should be viewed as an integral part of scholarly career development.

Students entering a doctoral program may plan for the period of the program, say four years. However, the planning horizon should be about ten years. The time schedule below does not fit all universities but is common. A typical rule is that a new assistant professor (using North American terminology) is evaluated for reappointment and tenure in the sixth year. If not reappointed, the seventh year is the last year at that institution.

Years	
1	Course work and initial research experiences
2	Course work, research experiences, selection of dissertation topic
3	Work on dissertation
4	Completion of dissertation

5	Beginning scholarly career with academic appointment
6–9	Scholarly career with research and publications
10	Review of performance in research, teaching, and service to decide on reappointment and tenure

The implications of the sixth year review is that only the work done during the doctoral program plus work done during the first five years in a position have an impact on the evaluation. If a student starts a new research program unrelated to the dissertation during the second year of an appointment (second year because it takes time to settle in a new position), there is only a four-year period to do the research and get it published. This is a short time period.

A more productive approach is to select a dissertation topic that is part of a research stream with potential topics for ten years or more. (New research streams may emerge to replace this initial stream by the end of the ten-year period.) When the dissertation is completed, it is only the first major topic in the research stream. Other topics can be started with little delay. They benefit from the extensive work done for the dissertation. The accumulated expertise improves the work. It provides the basis for research funding requests. The research results of dissertation plus another five years of research in related topics make a coherent contribution as a stream of research. New ideas and new research streams may emerge during this period, but the basic evidence of competence as a scholar and researcher is the stream that began with the dissertation.

The idea is to think of the dissertation as one step in a stream of research. The stream fits within an area of interest within an academic field. In other words:

Academic Field
  Area of Interest Within Academic Field
    Stream of Research Within Broad Area
      Dissertation as One Specific Topic Within Stream

As an example,

Academic Field is **Management**
Area of Interest is **Organization Structure**
Stream of Research is **Effect of Information
Technology on Organization Structure**
Dissertation as One Specific Topic is **Effect of
Information Technology on Span of Control**

The advantages of this approach are improved productivity as a scholar, increased opportunity for making a cumulative impact (reputation) in an area of interest, and guidance in planning the courses and research experiences in the first two years of a doctoral program. This plan allows preliminary work to be performed early. Some of this work may be publishable. For example, a student may prepare the following papers during dissertation work and present them at conferences and publish them in conference proceedings or regular, refereed research journals.

Year	
1	Prepare a paper analyzing existing thought and research in an area of interest
	Prepare a paper analyzing existing thought and research in a proposed stream of research
2	Prepare a paper proposing a set of research topics for the stream of research
	Do an exploratory study and present results at a conference
3	Prepare a paper proposing improved theory and research for the stream
4	Prepare a paper describing the dissertation research and its results

There are competitive academic market conditions supporting this approach. In a competitive market, those students who have demonstrated ability to do research and publish results have an advantage over students who are completing a dissertation as their first work and have not published anything.

Summary

This chapter provides concepts that are useful in understanding the nature of the dissertation project, which is defined in terms of knowledge work. Principles of productivity for knowledge work are directly applicable to the doctoral dissertation and also to ongoing work as a scholar. The five major ways to improve productivity in doing a dissertation are applied in the systematic approach described in the book:

- *Improve motivation.* The approach divides and structures individual activities. It provides for completion motivation by breaking the dissertation project into small subtasks. The subtasks allow motivational feedback from advisor and committee members.
- *Improve task management.* The approach emphasizes planning (a cognitive bargain), scheduling activities to reduce unproductive delays in the work and in relations with advisor and committee members, improving synergy among activities, scheduling for most productive utilization of time and energy, and applying stopping rules.
- *Conserve attention.* The approach emphasizes methods of conserving the time and mental effort of advisor and committee members in commenting on ideas, proposals, progress reports, and chapters. It also stresses the importance of selecting patterns and structures early in the process so they can be automatic, developing key expertise to reduce effort, and reducing design effort by using existing patterns for format and structure of a dissertation.
- *Reduce errors and omissions.* The approach indicates the value of methods for careful work and documentation along with selection, learning, and use of procedures that will reduce "first-time" errors and omissions.

- *Eliminate redundant processes.* Planning is emphasized in the approach. This includes early selection of procedures and formats to reduce rework and eliminate redundant processes. There is a flow of work from ideas to proposal to dissertation that builds on prior work and reduces redundant processes.

Two additional concepts were discussed in the chapter. The first was the role of the dissertation as a major research project for those beginning their academic career; the second was the dissertation as a midcareer demonstration of scholarly ability. These concepts explain many of the differences in doctoral programs in different countries.

CHAPTER 4

The Selection of an Advisor and a Dissertation Committee

An advisor is a faculty member who supervises the work of a doctoral student and is primarily responsible for mentoring and guiding the student in doing good work that will be accepted as a dissertation. Terminology may vary with different universities and structural arrangements may differ, but the basic concept is a faculty member who advises, sponsors, and mentors a doctoral student.

The advisor has significant power and influence in determining whether or not a candidate shall be allowed to continue in the doctoral program. An advisor's guidance is usually a significant factor affecting the quality of the final dissertation. The selection of the advisor is therefore an important decision.

At some universities, advisors and committees are arbitrarily assigned. A candidate can usually work satisfactorily with most advisors and most committees. But in those cases where the candidate is able to influence the selection of the advisor and the committee, the student should seek to select the advisor and the committee that will provide the best assistance.

The Ideal Relationship

The ideal advisor for a candidate has the following characteristics:

1. The advisor is interested in the topic.
2. The advisor is competent to advise on the topic. This means that the advisor is capable of reviewing the research and giving sound advice. This ideally includes advisor research on similiar or related topics and use of similar research methods
3. The advisor has a reasonable level of expectations regarding what a student can and should accomplish in a doctoral dissertation.
4. The advisor reads and comments on dissertation documents within a reasonable time period.
5. The advisor is consistant regarding requirements and advice and does not constantly add requirements or change advice already given.
6. The advisor has personal integrity and views the advisor role as an important responsibility, deserving of a faculty member's attention.
7. The advisor is interested in the candidate as a person and is interested in the candidate's welfare, both as a person and as a scholar.

The advisor gives guidance and advice, acts as sponsor with the committee, and is the one most able to protect the candidate from possible unfair demands by the dissertation committee. Therefore, a mutual respect is needed that allows the candidate to trust the advisor and the advisor to have confidence in the student. A candidate who does a good dissertation is a credit to the advisor. The advisor can take pride in the good work of advisees. Therefore, an advisor favors a candidate who will do a good job.

The rest of the dissertation committee is important because they function in approving the dissertation. They can also be of great assistance in planning the dissertation and performing the research. The ideal committee will provide skills supportive to the candidate. A student doing an investigation involving human behavior may have one committee member interested and competent in the behavioral sciences and perhaps another in the statistical analysis of data. The criteria for a committee member are similar to those of an advisor, but the committee member should, if possible, complement the advisor. The advisor must work with the committee and must feel comfortable with them. A student who has the option of suggesting a committee should do so, but should be prepared to suggest alternative members in order to provide some flexibility for the advisor proposing the committee.

The committee and, especially, the advisor are likely to be important in facilitating a candidate's career. Normally, the best assistance in obtaining an academic position comes from an advisor and the rest of the committee. Joint research and publishing with the advisor or others on the committee are factors that may establish a significant professional relationship and continuing friendship.

The personal relationship between faculty and the doctoral candidate should be that of senior and junior colleague. The dissertation marks the last major step toward independent professional status. However, the dissertation is the candidate's, not the advisor's or the committee's, dissertation.

Analyzing Alternative Advisors and Committee Members

If an advisor and a committee are assigned to a candidate, then an analysis is unnecessary. But in most cases, the candidate has considerable latitude in proposing a committee. While there is no way to be certain that the best advisor has been chosen, some factors, such as the following, can provide evidence for the decision process.

1. *Past performance with other candidates.* In a large department of 20 professors authorized to be advisors, the doctoral candidates will tend to cluster around four or five professors who have shown an interest and an ability in assisting candidates. In considering potential advisors, a recent past record of successful candidates is an important plus factor. The recency of the record may be important because some professors change in their orientation to students. The criteria should be approached cautiously, however, because some professors have not had the opportunity to have doctoral advisees, so these criteria are not applicable to them.

2. *Interest and competence in topic area or research methodology.* The interest of a prospective advisor does not have to be specific to the candidate's topic, but it should include the general area and the research methodology being used. Competence is the ability to understand a candidate's plan and project, in order to provide sound advice.

3. *Personality and personal characteristics.* Are the personalities of the candidate and the advisor compatible? Does the advisor demonstrate integrity in criticism? Does the advisor demonstrate personal integrity in dealings with students and advisees? Discussion with a faculty member's current candidates can be helpful in assessing an advisor's "style," manner of providing support, capacity to offer critical assistance, and availability.

4. *Response characteristics.* An advisor may be good, but may procrastinate reading and commenting on student materials. This may be due to personal habits or an excessive overall workload.

It is impossible to quantify the process or the factors that are important in selecting an advisor. Candidates should review the factors and decide their importance in their situation, keeping in mind the goal of timely completion.

Because of the different dynamics in the interactions between doctoral students and advisors, one student may like and appreciate certain advisor behaviors that another student finds difficult. For example, some students may view an advisor who specifies the research topic for the student based on the advisor's research program as providing excellent direction and removing uncertainty in topic selection; other students may find this constraining and limiting to student creativity and research contribution. At the extremes, a faculty member who is willing to supervise any topic without regard to ability for the opportunity to mentor and advise is not a good advisor, nor is one who overspecifies and overcontrols because this behavior does not allow a student to develop as an independent scholar.

The committee members may also be evaluated in much the same way. The competence and interest characteristics of potential committee members are significant. Two major criteria for selection are the assistance a proposed committee member is likely to provide to the candidate and the advisor's feeling as to how the proposed committee member will function in the committee.

The Ideal Candidate

The previous discussion described the ideal advisor. The ideal candidate, from the standpoint of the advisor and the committee, is one with whom they feel they can be effective. They generally want a candidate

1. who will do a good dissertation in a reasonable time that they can be proud to sign;
2. who shows initiative, but accepts guidance and follows through on suggestions;
3. who is organized, uses the committee's time effectively, and is also reasonable in the demands on their time;
4. who has personal integrity.

Candidates show these characteristics by the way they interact with the advisor and the committee. If predissertation activities have provided good interaction with the faculty members (described in the next chapter), a good relationship may already have been established. In other cases, candidates give indicators of future performance by the way they approach the dissertation project.

Professors will be much more willing to serve on a committee if the candidate demonstrates that the time demands will be reasonable, that their time will be used effectively, and that a good dissertation will result. Students who follow the systematic management approach are likely to demonstrate that they meet these criteria.

CHAPTER 5

Predissertation Development Activities

Students commonly wait until they have completed all requirements except the dissertation before seriously considering the dissertation topic. The difficulty with this approach is that there are many dissertation topics that they cannot then handle because they have not had the proper background in terms of course work or other study. This chapter proposes a plan in which the student selects the general area of the dissertation while course work is being planned. The candidate then uses the courses to do predissertation development. This ensures that the necessary course work and statistical and mathematical tools needed for the dissertation project will be available. The benefits from early selection of a topic are also applicable to a master's thesis.

Not all students are able to do the predissertation development activities proposed in the chapter. Some students do not make a commitment to the doctorate until their course work has begun. Other students have difficulty in deciding on a general area for scholarly inquiry. Then, some students find it difficult to think about a dissertation when they are concentrating on completing the course work, passing the qualifying examinations, and meeting other requirements. However, students who cannot do all of the predissertation development activities should, as a minimum, establish dissertation topic files early in their doctoral work.

Selection of General Area for Investigation

The basis for the predissertation development activities is early selection of the topic area for the dissertation. Topic area in this case is usually large and general. For example, a student in management might select planning as a general area for investigation. Or the topic may be narrowed to strategic planning. No attempt is made at this time to narrow the general area into a thesis topic. With a tentative selection of a general area for investigation, the student should take the earliest opportunity to do some investigation and reading in the area, giving special attention to the type of research skills that were necessary for the research being reviewed as well as the general background that would be useful for someone doing research in the area.

EXAMPLE 1: In the case of planning, the student might find that some research has used survey and interviewing techniques to obtain data about current practices in government and industry, while other investigations have used computer simulation. The investigations have generally required an understanding of the psychological nature of humans in a planning situation. This knowledge can be useful in planning course work in psychology.

EXAMPLE 2: A student interested in the outcomes of counseling and psychotherapy might discover that assessment has been done using field research (actual therapy cases), analogue studies (simulated laboratory counseling), and basic psychological laboratory research. The student might also find that there was a need to show correspondence between particular counseling strategies and particular outcomes as well as to link counselor personality traits and client problems. Such awareness can be useful in the selection of course work including the needed methodological statistical design courses.

Course Work in Predissertation Development

Most students, when planning their course work for the doctorate, have a number of both required and optional courses.

The choice of a minor, or supporting, program is generally left to the student. Rather than haphazardly selecting a minor, the student should consider the areas that will be needed as support for a future dissertation project and future research plans. For instance, a student who is interested in planning and already has reasonable skills in quantitative techniques, such as simulation, might decide to emphasize certain survey techniques for data collection in the research methodology course. That student should take a minor in psychology, sociology, or some set of courses that support an understanding of human behavior in organizations.

The student can use the courses to help solidify ideas and get suggestions for ways to approach the dissertation topics. For example, while proceeding with course work, the student may perceive that there will be a need to collect data from organizations. While taking a course in survey methodology, the candidate might use course problems in formulating a survey plan for possible use in the dissertation research. If the course requires a project, the student might develop a test of a possible data collection plan for the class project. The student might take a course in psychology that discusses experiments showing risk-aversion tendencies in humans and the relationship to human behavior in planning situations. A paper or other project in the course might provide an opportunity for the student to explore the relevance of this research to the general area of dissertation interest.

The use of course work in predissertation development has another advantage. The student is able to come in contact with potential committee members. The student becomes acquainted with professors in classroom situations and learns their interests. In connection with papers and other projects required for class, the student is able to discuss the dissertation area. The course instructors might make useful suggestions on how the student could structure a research project in the area.

Dissertation Ideas File

Dissertation ideas occur at strange times—while brushing teeth, watching a movie, or working on an unrelated course problem. The wise student will immediately write down and file each idea that seems remotely worthwhile. A student will commonly have dissertation ideas while reading journal articles or listening to talks. Alternative research plans often come to mind when reading research results. If the topic is a result of a suggestion made in a journal article, this should be carefully referenced so that the reference will not have to be searched a second time. All of these ideas should be kept in a dissertation idea file, which may simply consist of a notebook or a set of file folders. Every six months or so, ideas can be organized into a skeleton outline, known as the topic analysis form (to be presented in Chapter 8). This outline form indicates the general topic or the hypothesis, the importance of the topic, the theory base, the general methodology, the possible outcomes, and the contribution to knowledge. The purpose of putting the ideas in this form is to start thinking about dissertation topics in an organized way. However, the main thing is to build up a file of interesting topics. Investigation and selection can be done later.

Risks and Alternatives

There appear to be substantial advantages in thinking ahead to the dissertation. If it is possible to select a general area for investigation, then course work should support that topic. Work within the courses should be used as much as possible. The student should become acquainted with faculty members who have interests that would support the dissertation. If the dissertation develops as anticipated, predissertation development activities are likely to be very valuable, reduce the total time for the dissertation, and allow improvement in the quality of the dissertation. However, there is some risk in this strategy.

The general area selected early in doctoral work may not become the area of the dissertation. The candidate may arrange a program around one general area and find that it does not support the final topic. To balance the benefits and the risks, students should generally take a good, solid set of courses related to doctoral research, but include some courses that support the general area tentatively chosen. The assigned papers and projects in course work should still be used as opportunities to investigate potential dissertation topics or to do preliminary work.

CHAPTER **6**

The Selection of a Dissertation Topic

Most students have a difficult time visualizing a doctoral dissertation (or master's thesis). The discussion of contribution to knowledge and scope of topics seems abstract at first. The standard of quality is so vague as to be meaningless. The student is likely to get responses such as the following:

Question	Typical Answer
What are the quality standards?	High!
How long does a dissertation have to be?	Long enough to develop the subject properly!
How exhaustive should the literature survey be?	Fairly exhaustive!

Rather than trying to define quality, length, style, and other requirements, the student should examine a set of dissertations (or master's theses). Dissertations (and some master's theses) for each university are generally filed in the library. Dissertations accepted by other universities may be obtained (1) from those universities via interlibrary loan, or (2) from University Microfilms, in Ann Arbor, Michigan (for American and some European dissertations); abstracts of dissertations are published in *Dissertation Abstracts International*, a reference generally available in a research library or through on-line computer database searches. Master's theses from other universities may usually be obtained through interlibrary loan if the awarding university requires a copy to be placed in the library (which many do not require).

A student might also examine some of the following:
1. Award-winning dissertations in the candidate's field or related fields
2. Recent dissertations in the selected field at various universities
3. Good recent dissertations as suggested by faculty in the department
4. The best dissertations suggested by the advisor

In reading dissertations, the student should begin to formulate a general understanding of the structure and scope of a dissertation, and the meaning of *contribution to knowledge* as applied to doctoral dissertations. Discussions with other students, faculty, and the advisor are also helpful.[1]

Characteristics of a Good Dissertation Topic

No dissertation topic is perfect. However, in searching for a topic, certain important characteristics should be kept in mind:
1. Research needed and interesting
2. Theory base for research
3. Amenable to research methods
4. Achievable in reasonable time
5. Symmetry of potential outcomes
6. Matches student capabilities and interest
7. Attractive for funding
8. Area for professional development

The dissertation must make a contribution to knowledge, but this important element will be discussed in a separate section of the chapter.

RESEARCH NEEDED AND INTERESTING

There should be a need for the research, and it should be significant or important; otherwise, the research should not be

---

[1]*See also* M. M. Chambers, "Selection, Definition and Delimitation of a Doctoral Research Problem," *Phi Delta Kappan*, 42 (3) (1963): 71–73.

conducted. This does not mean that the results must have immediate application, but rather that the topic should not be trivial or of little importance. The student should also feel the problem is important and worthwhile because there will be periods of routine work, and enthusiasm for the project helps to keep it moving during such times. The need to understand the nature of things is the motivation for much research that has no immediate use, but there should be some need, importance, or significance in knowing the result. For example, a student might think about research on the color preferences of school principals. It is possible to get such data and analyze it, but the results are probably neither important nor interesting.

THEORY BASE FOR RESEARCH

The theory base or theory foundation provides the basis for a contribution. Because there may be several possibilities for theory base, it should be selected and justified based on research aims or purposes. If a question or problem cannot be related to theory or concepts, research is not likely to make a contribution. The importance of a theory base is rooted in the cycle of knowledge development. Observations lead to theory to classify, explain, and predict the observations. The theory leads to questions about the behavior or actions being observed. Theory-based research defines expected outcomes and the variables associated with them. The theory base provides a reason for expecting to find certain results. Research provides evidence for or against the theory-based expectations. Results that are contrary to the theory suggest the need to modify the theory; results as expected provide support or further explanation for the theory.

The theory base may be part of the common theories used in the field of study, or it may come from other disciplines. For example, the theory base for a dissertation on software development practices may come from cognitive science and economics. The theory base is important in formulating research propositions and procedures; it can also be useful in identifying and developing research topics.

If no theory base can be identified, the topic should be rejected. Examples of topics that would be rejected as having no theory base are "The influence of the stars on human behavior" and "The effect of human expectations on payoffs of gambling devices." There is no theory base that explains why the stars should have any influence on human behavior, and there is no theory that would predict how human expectations can affect mechanical devices used in gambling. Note, however, that there is theory that explains why humans might believe the stars have an influence or believe that expectations might influence gambling devices, so propositions related to researching human behavior in these cases might be acceptable.

AMENABLE TO RESEARCH METHODS

The topic needs to be feasible regarding both availability of data and availability of tools for analysis. There are many interesting problems that cannot be researched because no suitable research methods exist, or data cannot be obtained. Some research methods may be unacceptable because of government or university regulations. For example, the U.S. Department of Health, Education and Welfare requires universities to establish and police guidelines for research involving human subjects. It should also be noted that some research methods are beyond the capabilities of students because of technical, cost, or time requirements. A topic that is probably not amenable to doctoral research is a proposal to study the causes of the United States' failure to win the Vietnam war. The number of factors that impinged on that particular set of events was large and included the decisions made by several presidents over a 20-year period. The interrelatedness of these complex events would be indeterminable during the period of time, and with the resources normally available to a Ph.D. candidate.

ACHIEVABLE IN REASONABLE TIME

The normal amount of required time for a doctoral thesis probably varies from university to university. However, rather than leaving "reasonable time" completely undefined, some rough estimates will be presented, which students can translate to the situation of their university.

The range of time for most dissertations is probably from twelve to twenty work months, the elapsed time usually being longer because of part-time work and similar delays. The exploratory investigation, definition of problem, and writing normally take about half of the total time. This rough computation suggests that the running of experiments, data collection, data analysis, theory formulation, and other activities, should be achievable in from 6 to 10 work months (probably close to 6). Because many activities occur in parallel (E.G., writing of chapter on prior research while collecting data), the time span over which data collection, analysis, and other activities can occur may be from 8 to 12 months. A student may wish to select a topic having a longer time requirement, but should do so with an awareness of the consequences for the date of completion. An illustration of a topic that does not meet the completion time criterion is a dissertation topic that proposes to study the development of college students from the freshman to senior years. This is a study that would have to extend over four or more years and, therefore, normally would not be suitable as a dissertation topic. Time limitations may sometimes be overcome by alternative research designs. In the above example, the topic may be studied in a shorter time by taking measurements for two groups that are matched by characteristics, one group consisting of freshman students, the other group composed of senior students. However, such cross-sectioned studies have severe limitations, resulting from potentially different subject characteristics that develop over time, dropouts from college, and different selection criteria.

SYMMETRY OF POTENTIAL OUTCOMES

A research project will typically have more than one potential outcome. For example, a research experiment may fail to disprove the null hypothesis, it may disprove it, or it may be inconclusive. An algorithm for solving a class of problems will either work or not work.

The ideal dissertation topic is one in which (given a careful methodology) any of the potential outcomes would be satisfactory in terms of dissertation acceptability. For example, a student may have a hypothesis that two alternative teaching methodologies will have differential outcomes. If the experiment is well conducted and the research design and statistical procedures are appropriate, then confirming the hypothesis is an important result, with implications for teaching a particular subject matter. However, the opposite is also interesting. If it is shown that neither teaching method has a clear advantage over the other, this conclusion is just as important, because either method can be used, depending on considerations other than outcomes.

As an example of nonsymmetrical outcomes, a hypothesis that says that one can predict decision-making style from characteristics of an executive turns out to be important in only one case. If this hypothesis is confirmed and the prediction can be made with reasonable accuracy, the result is interesting. But suppose there is to be no correlation. This is not nearly as interesting, and it probably would not be a significant contribution.

This lack of symmetry applies to most dissertations involving new algorithms or solutions procedures. If the algorithm is found, there is a good dissertation. If no algorithm is found, a contribution has not been made. Note, however, that if a solution method has been proposed by one or more authorities but not proved, then a dissertation might proceed to prove or disprove that this algorithm can be used. Then, proving that the algorithm is feasible or showing that it does not work in a particular situation (because it was thought to be feasible) is a contribution to knowledge.

MATCHES STUDENT CAPABILITIES AND INTEREST

A topic should match the capabilities and interest of the student. A student who has strong capabilities in the behavioral sciences and low mathematical capabilities should not choose a mathematical dissertation involving proofs and algorithms, even though it might otherwise be a good topic. A student with strong mathematical capabilities and little interest or training in behavioral science should not choose a topic that depends for its success on high ability and training in that field.

ATTRACTIVE FOR FUNDING

In a pure scholarly sense, funding should not be a consideration. But most students who are doing dissertation research have a sufficiently broad range of possibilities that they can choose among alternatives. When selecting among alternatives, a student might consider the likelihood that each topic will attract the necessary funding. Topics that are current and have some unusual approach are usually most likely to obtain funding. Current faculty research grants commonly provide dissertation research support for topics that fit the purpose of the grant.

AREA FOR PROFESSIONAL DEVELOPMENT

A dissertation may either be the beginning of research on a topic or the end. A student puts a significant amount of work into a dissertation topic and, therefore, becomes one of the most knowledgeable scholars on that subject. If there is likely to be a continuing interest, either academically or otherwise on the topic, then a student can continue to maintin scholarly capability in the area and continue to be a significant authority on the subject. The dissertation can, therfore, be a career stepping stone if the selected topic provides development in areas in which the student is likely to work. Because there is a great deal of risk in the dissertation research, a student will usually select a topic in an area that is characterized by some prior research, rather than a completely new area for research. "Exploratory" research is usually too underdefined to allow a student to demonstrate competency, and it often results in asymmetrical results. On the other hand, candidates need to avoid overworked areas where they would be merely reworking someone else's ideas and not making a contribution of their own.

Sources of Potential Topics

A student generally has some idea of one or more general areas in which to search for a topic. There are several fruitful sources for identifying potential dissertation topics.

1. *Current events.* The current events or popular journals often describe problems relating to social welfare, business, economics, education, and government before the scholarly journals in a field recognize them as problems requiring research. One reason for this is the delay in publication by many scholarly journals (a one-year delay after acceptance is not unusual). For example, it was clear from the news media that pornography would be a social issue well before the presidential commission on pornography was appointed. A doctoral student in sociology, in the early 1960s, would have been able to identify the emerging problem from the news media (and perhaps from scholarly journals as well).

2. *Suggestions for research from past dissertations.* A student who has an interest in an area should obtain copies of dissertations that have been written in the area. The method of search is presented later in this chapter. Writers of dissertations commonly describe further research that needs to be done. The suggestions are potentially valuable because they come from persons who have done research in the area.

3. *Suggestions for research by authorities in the field.* Generally, there are a few well-known authorities in a field,

and they often comment on the need for research in articles or speeches. In many cases, an article or a committee report will be issued specifically on the need for research in an area.

4. *Expressions of need for research by practitioners in a field.* In the field of management, a well-known and well-regarded manager may describe the areas where he or she feels there is insufficient evidence on which to base decision making. These suggestions must be viewed cautiously because the practitioners are commonly not aware of research that has been done. However, this provides a good starting point for further investigation.

5. *Generally accepted but unproved suppositions.* Every field of knowledge or endeavor has a large number of suppositions or accepted ideas that no one has ever bothered to test or validate. For example, one highly regarded and widely used text in reading and study skills proposed a system for studying that was quoted for 20 years but never systematically tested. Subsequent tests of the method failed to find any evidence for its assertions. Indeed, evidence was found for a much simpler technique that could be taught more easily with more effective results.

6. *Unproved or weakly proved assertions by an authority in the field.* Authorities in the field frequently will make unproved or poorly proved assertions. These need to be tested and subjected to further analysis. For example, a well-known researcher may assert that capital-budgeting techniques are used as a control mechanism, rather than as the basis for decision making. He may say that he has never seen a company that actually used them for decision-making purposes. Therefore, he reasons, the extreme emphasis on capital-budgeting techniques and on the refining of the techniques is misplaced. This assertion by an authority in the field can obviously be proved or disproved by accumulating evidence from research.

7. *Theories and concepts without supporting research.* When theories or conceptual frameworks are developed, they generally have some supporting research but may be weakly or incompletely supported, providing an opportunity for research. In other cases, the theory does not seem to work well. These instances provide research questions. Is the theory incomplete or wrong? Research can be designed to provide evidence on the completeness or usefulness of the theory.

8. *Different approaches to testing of important results.* If a researcher has reported interesting results with one research technique and a given research population, a doctoral student may consider replicating the experiment, altering either the research technique or the research population. One researcher might study consumer reaction to price changes by bringing consumers into a laboratory setting where they are asked to rate the importance of price differences on the purchase decision. Another researcher might replicate the essence of the experiment but use after-purchase interviews with consumers who have just made a purchase, thereby changing the experimental technique. In another experiment, one researcher might conduct a simulation using college students to find that attitude change is highly correlated with the physical attractiveness of the influencer. Such a simulation conducted with college students can be replicated using middle-aged consumers' attitudes toward particular market products or workers' attitudes toward political issues. When significant results are obtained in the college laboratory using students, it is useful to replicate the experiment in the real environment or population to determine if the results still hold. There is some evidence to suggest that the artificiality of students as subjects may induce incorrect results.

The Contribution of a Dissertation

A requirement for almost all doctoral dissertations is that they make a contribution to knowledge; however, it is difficult to define precisely the meaning of the term *contribution to knowledge*. What is acceptable at one university might not be acceptable at another. One advisor might accept what another may reject. The dissertation should be based on a significant question, problem, or hypothesis. The work should be original and should relate to, explain, solve, or add proof to the question, problem or hypothesis. The research adds to knowledge and usually results in the formation of generalizations. The additive contribution of a dissertation may arise from

1. new or improved evidence;
2. new or improved methodology;
3. new or improved analysis;
4. new or improved concepts or theories.

The contribution of a dissertation may be based on more than one of these. For example, a dissertation might develop some theory, obtain empirical data, and integrate the two.

NEW OR IMPROVED EVIDENCE

The evidence in a dissertation may disprove or support a concept, theory, or model. Evidence may disprove or support a hypothesis, or it may add to the understanding of a process. Major questions regarding evidence are

How were the data collected?

How were the data analyzed?

The evidence may be collected by an experiment, simulation, observations, questionnaire, interviews, or measurements. A major question regarding such evidence is the method by which it was obtained. If a researcher asks, "Are you prejudiced?" and if 95 percent of the respondents say "No," does this provide solid evidence? Almost certainly not because most people, prejudiced or not, will tend to answer no. The technique is faulty, so the results are faulty.

The method of analysis is likewise significant. Reporting the means of badly skewed distributions is misleading; not providing the changes in the variance of a distribution may lead to wrong conclusions. For example, in the field of psychotherapy outcome, research was reported for years in terms of mean changes. When one researcher began to examine changes in variance he discovered that some patients got worse and some got better. Results that had looked like "no change" now had to be examined for "deterioration" effects as well as gains.

NEW OR IMPROVED METHODOLOGY

The contribution can be a new or improved solution or analysis procedure (such as a new statistical procedure) or a new or improved research methodology (such as a new method for obtaining data on personality disorders). Showing the benefit of applying a known procedure in a new way may also be a contribution.

Improvement from a new or changed methodology or solution procedure should be significant. For example, a dissertation showing that a new solution algorithm for correlation coefficients can reduce errors in the result at the fourth decimal place is not worthy of acceptance as a doctoral dissertation. Correlation coefficients are rarely significant beyond two places, if that. However, if the new solution procedure should be applied to significant computational problems, it might be a contribution.

Quantitative solution procedures can be demonstrated by proofs and examples. Other solution procedures may need to be supplemented by evidence of their efficacy. For example, a student may propose (and support with conceptual reasoning) a new solution procedure for developing a strategic plan for an organization (such as a business). Unless there is supporting evidence, the mere assertion that this is a successful solution procedure is probably not sufficient. A single-case example may often be sufficient to demonstrate its feasibility, but testing its relative efficacy compared to other methods is probably another dissertation topic and may be left for another researcher.

NEW OR IMPROVED ANALYSIS

Analysis may be based on existing evidence or include new data. The following are some examples of types of analysis.

1. *Historical analysis.* Ideas or historical forces are developed. An example is an economic interpretation of the American Revolution.
2. *Analysis of implications of a current development in a field.* An example is an analysis of the impact of transaction analysis on counseling.
3. *Comparative analysis.* Theories, methodologies, or systems are compared. An example is a comparison of management theory in capitalist and socialist environments.
4. *Analysis of an existing theory or concept and its implications.* An example is an analysis of the theory of cognitive dissonance.

The method of analysis may be important. There are usually generally accepted methods in a field. For example, there are methods for historical analysis and for analysis of economic theories as well as methods for experimental analysis. In other cases there are no generally accepted approaches. While there may be a need to innovate, the student may find it useful to consider applying known techniques accepted as valid in other fields before embarking on untried methods of analysis.

NEW OR IMPROVED CONCEPTS OR THEORIES

Concepts, theories, or models are developed to explain phenomena in a field or to provide structure or framework to knowledge in a field. An entirely new concept, theory, or model may be developed, or an existing concept, theory, or model may be enlarged or extended. In such a concept or theory dissertation, it is usually desirable to illustrate how the theory, concept, or model can be used to explain, predict, or understand. Concepts or theories may be developed as part of quantitative or qualitative dissertation research. An example is development of grounded theory in which theory is based on observations and data. This approach to a theory contribution is consistent with the normal scope of a doctoral dissertation.

Concept and theory contributions may be made by analyzing existing theory relative to research results and suggesting a modified set of concepts or theory, or by developing models, frameworks, concepts, and theories based on logic or application of concepts and theories from other fields. Such theory development usually benefits from researcher experience and maturity. Acceptance of a contribution may be problematic because the criteria for accepting theory are less well defined than the criteria for quantitative or qualitative research. Because dissertations that focus on modifying existing theory or a theory development process have a high level of uncertainty relative to achieving a recognized contribution, such dissertations should probably not be selected unless there are strong reasons supporting them.

Research Methodology Issues in Topic Selection

A student doing a dissertation topic exploration will usually explore more than one topic and each topic may be amenable to more than one research methodology. The methodology may be an important consideration in selecting a topic. When a topic is selected, the best methodology may be obvious, but often there are alternative methodologies that are about equal. Important issues relative to the methodology to be selected are the problem, methods usually used in an academic field, methodology support available, and career development considerations.

RESEARCH METHODOLOGY AND RESEARCH PROBLEM

The research methodology should fit the research problem, research aims, and theory base. However, more than one methodology can be applied to most problems. Methodology selection is therefore part of topic selection. In discussions of research, sets of terms are often used to distinguish research methods: Examples are experimental versus descriptive, quantitative versus qualitative, and positivist versus postpositivist. These reflect not only ways of doing research but also strongly held opinions about the value of evidence and interpretations achieved by the methods.

- *Experimental versus descriptive.* This is a dichotomy between research that obtains evidence by conducting experiments that manipulate one or more conditions in order to measure the effect on a dependent variable and research that obtains descriptive data on conditions as they exist and explains them.

- *Quantitative versus qualitative.* Quantitative data is obtained by instruments such as questionnaires, measurements of responses to stimuli, and financial or economic reports. The analysis typically employs statistical techniques such as regression, variance analysis, and estimation. Conceptually, the quantitative researcher is independent of the phenomena and the measurements. Qualitative research employs interviews and observations. The researcher may be an uninvolved observer or a participant observer. From a rich set of observations, the research develops interpretations. The interpretations either relate to theory or provide a basis for developing theory.

- *Positivist versus postpositivist.* The scientific method is positivist: A problem is identified, data are collected, and hypotheses are formulated and empirically tested. There is a strong positivist, quantitative research tradition in the sciences. Inferential statistics are employed to determine the likelihood that results differ from chance results. Many problems, especially in the social sciences and humanities, do not lend themselves to hypothesis testing and statistical analysis. Other methods of collecting and analyzing data reflect the richness of complex human situations and allow the researcher to apply alternative interpretations or develop alternative theories. The orientation of the post-positivist approach is qualitative, rather than quantitative.

Most problems can be approached with experimental, quantitative, positivist methods, but research on some problems achieves more meaningful results with descriptive, qualitative, postpositivist, interpretive methods. Problems amenable to measurement of variables and theory-based formulation of meaningful hypotheses typically can be researched with positivist methods. Problems that reflect many difficult-to-measure variables and ill-defined relationships can usually be best understood with interpretive methods.

METHODS TYPICALLY USED IN AN ACADEMIC FIELD

Selection of a topic may be influenced by methodology based on how amenable the topic is to research methods usually employed in the field. Some fields are narrow in their choice of research methods; others are open and accept a wide range of methods. Understanding a field's research tradition is useful background to selecting a topic and research method for a dissertation. If a method is typically employed, there are three reasons for using it in a doctoral dissertation:

1. The dissertation research will be understood and appreciated by people in the academic field who employ the same method.
2. The dissertation result will be well supported by advisors and other faculty members in the field.

3. Using typical methods prepares a graduate for the important scholarly task of reviewing the work of other researchers who employ traditional methods.

Selecting a topic that employs a seldom-used research method may be appropriate, but a student should carefully consider the extra explanations and reasoning to get colleagues to accept methods that are not part of the common tradition of a field. Applying the "right" method may be worth the effort, but a student may have another option—doing a traditional dissertation and doing an alternative method as follow-on research. In many cases where both quantitative and qualitative methods may be used, a student can mix methods. For example, a student may collect data with questionnaires or other traditional instruments and analyze the results with traditional statistics. At the same time, the student may obtain qualitative, descriptive data from interviews and observations. The qualitative data are used to interpret and explain the quantitative results.

METHODOLOGY SUPPORT AVAILABLE

Methods typically employed in a field are usually well supported by advisors and other faculty members in the same field. However, even within a positivist or postpositivist tradition, there are a variety of different methods. For example, doing econometric analysis on a data set from a government economic database requires quantitative methods different from designing and conducting experiments with undergraduate students.

Persons doing doctoral dissertations should learn well the methodologies they apply and be able to explain their strengths and weaknesses. Statistical tests and qualitative analysis methods should not be employed blindly; the assumptions and limits should be explored and understood.

It is often desirable to have initial help with research methods. For example, a student doing structural equation models can benefit from expert advice until experience has been gained. It is helpful to try out a method with a small data set or a limited set of subjects in order to gain familiarity with the techniques. For example, a student planning to do ethnographic research should do a pilot project. If no help is available, the attractiveness of a method may be significantly reduced.

CAREER DEVELOPMENT CONSIDERATIONS

In the discussion of topic and research methodology, a student may be influenced in the choice of methodology by career development considerations. Is there a natural sequence of experience in research methods? This is a controversial point. However, the following observations suggest that, in the absence of strong considerations for postpositivist methods in the dissertation, using positivist methods in the dissertation is often better for career development.

- Positivist methods are well defined and therefore simpler to apply when the research is structured to use them. Interpretive methods are more difficult to apply, and there is less agreement on how to apply them properly.
- The rich, ambiguous data from interpretive research is more interesting and will therefore "drive out" the more limited, well-defined routines and procedures of positivist research. A good grounding in positivist research allows a research to go back and forth between the approaches; a poor grounding in positivist methods makes it difficult for a researcher to apply them well. The dissertation is usually sufficient to establish positivist credentials.
- A positivist dissertation is easier for colleagues to understand. It is easier to defend and to get results published. It therefore tends to be a better basis for early career development.
- Doing scholarly review of the work of others commonly requires positivist skills. A dissertation provides good grounding for this.

- A positivist dissertation provides the basis for a post-dissertation use of interpretive methods. The more narrow focus and discipline of positivist research suggests opportunities for interpretive research. The reverse is possible but not as likely to occur.

Good course work and experience reduce methodology constraints in selecting a topic. Students should gain familiarity with both positivist and interpretive methods in the depth appropriate to their field. With a good mix of short projects and exploratory analysis as part of a doctoral program, students can develop sufficient breadth of skill in both approaches to support a scholarly career. Either positivist or postpositivist methods can then be used for the dissertation.

Projects Not Generally Accepted as a Dissertation

It is generally agreed that literature surveys and descriptive compilations do not meet the contribution-to-knowledge requirement for the dissertation. State-of-the-art descriptions, no matter how well done, are generally not accepted. For example, a good textbook may be excellent in terms of contribution to teaching, but it is not generally considered to fulfill the contribution-to-knowledge requirement because textbooks tend to report the existing state of the art. A literature survey is included as part of most dissertations but this cannot be the main contribution of a dissertation.

A historical survey is not usually considered to be a contribution to knowledge unless accompanied by some analysis or testing of the historical ideas. For example, a historical survey of the development of some industry, such as the steel industry in the United States, might not be considered a satisfactory dissertation. However, if there is some underlying concept or analysis of the reason why the steel industry developed as it did, then this research would probably be accepted as a dissertation.

A description of American commerce during the American Revolution might be somewhat weak as a dissertation, but a description of American commerce as it relates to an economic interpretation of history might be considered to be a good dissertation. Multiple case studies may be used in developing concepts or explaining phenomena. There is some disagreement about the contribution made from single-case descriptions. In general, however, a case description of a single situation is probably not a satisfactory dissertation unless it is used in interpreting or developing an underlying structure, theory, or concept. In other words, a theory might be proposed, and then a single-case description might be used in developing or interpreting the underlying theory.

Development projects that apply known knowledge do not usually fulfill the requirements for dissertations (unless there are some comparative results, theory-based innovations, or significant demonstration of feasibility and value). Developing and installing a performance evaluation system in an organization such as a business, university, or government agency or writing a set of computer programs to do statistical analysis may be creative and worthwhile projects, but they do not represent doctoral dissertations—not because they lack substantial work or importance to the users, but because they represent development projects that do not add to knowledge. On the other hand, a dissertation project that proposes a behavioral theory to explain the use and nonuse of statistical packages, collects data showing the reasons packages are not used, develops a software package that overcomes these deficiencies, applies this software in an experimental setting, and then obtains statistics that show that the new approach does actually produce better results would probably be considered an acceptable dissertation. Note the primary difference, however: The software package in the second dissertation was merely a means of collecting data to prove an underlying concept.

7

Investigating Existing Knowledge on a Topic

An important part of the search for a topic is an investigation of existing knowledge and current research in the topic area. The investigation proceeds conceptually through the following three stages with increasing scope and depth.

1. Exploratory investigations, as part of the development and evaluation of possible topics in an area
2. Investigation in some depth, sufficient to support a formal research and dissertation proposal
3. Complete research that is described in the "literature/research" section of the dissertation

The literature/current research is a significant part not only of the topic selection, but also of the entire dissertation process. Because of the vast store of knowledge and the increasing rate at which knowledge is being accumulated, it is important that the researcher become efficient in literature search. A full treatise of this subject is beyond the scope of this book. However, a framework for initiating the search and a search strategy is suggested. The appendix includes a discussion of computer software in search processes.

Framework for Initializing the Search

Admundson[1] has suggested that a searcher consider both the *bibliographic chain* and the means of *bibliographic control*. A bibliographic chain refers to the channels through which an idea moves, as it progresses from a new idea to a formal study and eventually is incorporated into conventional knowledge. For example, a researcher may discover a new idea about a certain phenomenon while analyzing data on a project. The idea might be discussed with colleagues and students but not be known outside that close circle. Then the institution may allocate local "seed" money for investigation. If productive, external funding may be sought, and the idea captured in a grant proposal. When the formal research is completed, technical reports are prepared. Only when the idea is well formulated and initial confirmatory data are available is the idea published—often years after the work is completed. These published reports may appear first in conference proceedings and later in professional periodicals. When extensive research has been done a synthesis may appear in a monograph of some length. The more extensive research is often abstracted and collated with other related work and included in books. As those books are used, the idea becomes part of the body of knowledge in the field. The bibliographic chain explains why current research is difficult to locate—it is either not published or it appears in obscure technical reports and hard-to-find periodicals.

The World Wide Web is changing some of the traditional dynamics of publishing. Researchers may place papers on web pages long before they are published in journals. Some fields support electronic journals with reduced time for publication.

Bibliographic control refers to the various means by which a researcher locates the published and unpublished material related to an area of investigation. Figure 7-1 shows how bibliographic control interfaces with the bibliographic chain. The missing

---

[1]Colleen Admundson, Unpublished paper, 1973.

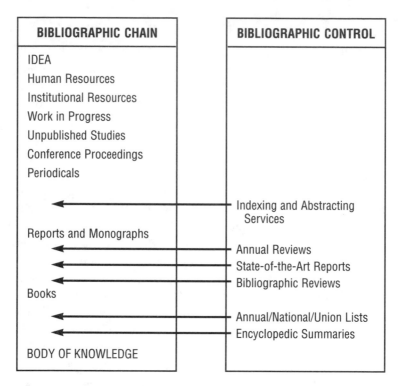

7-1. A bibliographic chain with bibliographic control (adapted from Admundson, Unpublished paper, 1973).

elements in Figure 7-1 are ways of locating early work in progress. These methods are mostly informal ways of engaging in a network of researchers. Seminars and colloquia are ways of finding out the most recent thinking of researchers in the field. Conferences and conventions provide opportunities for work in progress to be reported. Entering into the network is most effectively done through personal contacts with other researchers. These contacts can sometimes be made at conferences and conventions. Contacts are commonly made through e-mail or personal letters. While such personal contacts are difficult for doctoral students to make, they can be developed with some assistance from an advisor and some initiative on the part of the student. It should be obvious that the newer the ideas are, the more difficult they are to obtain. The more general and well-known information is easier to locate. Thus, finding the information needed to refine a research topic into a researchable idea, with the potential for contributing to the body of knowledge, will usually take considerable time and the candidate should allow for it.

Elements in a Search Strategy

A search of the literature related to a potential topic should not be a haphazard, random process. A search at the exploratory, proposal, or dissertation level will be most effective if the researcher plans a search strategy that is most likely to provide the depth and scope needed for a given stage of the dissertation. All search strategies assume that the researcher has become familiar with basic library guides to reference materials, computer databases, the World Wide Web, and search engines. Reference librarians may be consulted at appropriate points in a search.

It is important to a successful search strategy to identify useful descriptors or search terms. Start a list of terms you consider relevant. A thesaurus may be useful in developing alternative terms. A useful source of terms is the library subject headings in the U.S. Library of Congress, *Library of Congress Subject Headings*. The procedure is to look up a subject heading that best describes your research topic. The listing contains terms for which the subject heading is used, terms that broaden a search, related terms, "see also" terms, and narrower terms. Although the terms listed in the subject headings will not necessarily be the subject headings used in the periodical indexes or databases, they will help in locating books and other materials in the library.

The following elements can be combined into an appropriate search strategy.

1. *Published indexes.* Indexes for major topic areas can be searched manually for articles and books. For example,

there is a science citation index, an index of economics literature, and an index of psychological abstracts.

2. *CD-ROM reference databases.* The major reference indexes and a large variety of reference information is available on CD-ROMs. The CD-ROMs contain search software so that a researcher can locate items by key words, authors, and so forth. Relevant references and text may be copied to a researcher's diskette.

3. *On-line reference databases.* The major reference indexes to periodicals are available through various commercial on-line search services. In many cases, these can be accessed without charge through a university library. A researcher can also become a personal subscriber of an on-line service that provides access. Examples of on-line search services are BRS, Data-Star, Dialog, OCLC EPIC, and STN. Examples of databases are ERIC *(Education Resource Information Clearinghouse),* covering articles in 760 education journals; PsycLIT, covering reference journals in psychology and associated disciplines; and ABI Inform Global, providing selective indexing of about 1,000 journals in all business fields. These few examples illustrate the breadth of the databases and on-line services; a doctoral student in a subject area should become acquainted with the databases and on-line services relevant to the field.

The search in a specific academic field may have unique databases and search services. A general problem for doctoral students is searching for relevant dissertations on the topic being investigated. The next section will describe methods for doing dissertation searches.

INVESTIGATING PRIOR DOCTORAL RESEARCH

Recent doctoral dissertations are important in the topic search because the information is relatively current, not subject to long publication delays, and usually presented in detail and often includes an extensive bibliography, which can lead to additional resources. There are three published sources for doctoral dissertations. These sources are available on CD-ROM and through on-line search services.

The major source of information on doctoral dissertations is University Microfilms International (UMI Dissertation Services).[2] This company enables researchers to locate doctoral dissertations, acquire copies of dissertations, and obtain reprints of out-of-print scholarly books. The UMI database includes information on over 1,300,000 dissertations and theses, including information from over 250 institutions outside of the United States and Canada. Copies of items are available on microfiche, microfilm, and paper. The three most relevant publications of UMI are

1. *Dissertation Abstracts International,* a monthly publication of bibliographic citations and abstracts of doctoral dissertations. These are grouped by subject in three sections: humanities and social sciences, sciences and engineering, and institutions outside North America. Each section includes a key word index and an author index. The following data are included: title in original language, author's name, year of award, institution granting the degree, and UMI order number if relevant.

2. *Comprehensive Dissertation Index,* published since 1973, provides a key word index and an author index. Cumulative indexes cover the following periods: 1861–1972, 1973–1982, and 1983–1987.

3. *American Doctoral Dissertations,* a single volume, annual reference listing doctoral dissertations at American and Canadian institutions in a given academic year. Arranged by subject, by university within a subject, and by author within a university.

---

[2]When a dissertation has been located, a copy may be ordered from UMI. Ordering information is available in the publications. Further information can be obtained from UMI Dissertation Services, 300 North Zeeb Road, Ann Arbor, MI 48106-1346 U.S.A.

Dissertation abstracts are available on CD-ROM as *Dissertation Abstracts Ondisc* (DAO). This includes all bibliographic citations dating as far back as 1861. It has citations and fully searchable abstracts for titles published since July 1980. Many libraries have these CD-ROMs, but they are also available to individual researchers for a fee.

Dissertations Abstracts Online includes the entire dissertation database from 1861 and the full text of abstracts since July 1980. The database is available through on-line information search services, such as BRS, Data-Star, Dialog, OCLC EPIC, and STN. Researchers can order dissertation copies directly from some of the services.

When doing a manual search with the key word index, the index includes each significant word that appears in a title. Nonsignificant terms are not included. For example, a title of *An Inquiry into a Theory of Budgeting* will be indexed only under *Budgeting* because the other words are not good search terms. When a topic has been identified, a manual search can be used to locate dissertation titles that contain the terms. Why do any manual searching when a search can be done with computer search tools? The reason is that a manual search will help a researcher identify new terms and make a more complete computer search.

When doing searches with CD-ROM or on-line services, it is important to structure search terms to find relevant references but not include irrelevant items. The search procedures allow searching by author, title, date, school, and advisor. They also allow searching titles for key terms and abstracts for one or more terms. For example, *budgeting theory* can be used to find all dissertations with these two terms in this order in the title or in the abstract. It will not find *theory of budgeting*. To locate these two terms in either order or not adjacent, the search can request *budgeting* and *theory*. Additional specifications may be used and a researcher should learn these in order to be effective in doing a dissertation search.

CHAPTER 8

The Dissertation Proposal

The part of the dissertation project with which students seem to have the most difficulty is the preparation of a dissertation proposal outlining the research. It is a difficult activity, but one that is crucial in order to achieve the objective of timely completion. The proposal represents the blueprints for the dissertation. If the blueprints are clear and well done, the work can proceed with assurance; if incomplete and unclear, there is likely to be considerable misdirected effort.

The process of preparing a dissertation proposal is iterative. The student prepares a proposal and solicits reactions from advisor, committee, and colleagues. Based on their comments, the candidate prepares a revision. This is critiqued and a new revision is prepared. There may be an opportunity for the candidate to present the proposal in a seminar. The comments will result in further revision. The process should continue until the proposal is a clear, crisp definition of the research project. This approach to development of a dissertation proposal is equally effective in preparing a master's thesis proposal.

The use of topic analysis forms to outline topics is recommended in the formative stages when several alternative topics are being considered. When one topic is chosen, the topic analysis can be expanded into a dissertation proposal. The dissertation proposal then proceeds through several iterations until the research is sufficiently well defined for the proposal to be accepted.

The Topic Analysis

A student will usually consider several possible dissertation topics, or alternative approaches to the same problem, prior to selecting a final topic. The various topics should be analyzed as early as possible in terms of their suitability. A student who talks vaguely about doing a thesis on decision making in organizations does not yet have a dissertation topic because, within that general area, one might construct hundreds of possible dissertations. The problem is to identify several topics, prepare a topic analysis for each, and then choose the one that best meets the selection criteria. Unless the advisor has a specific problem in mind for the student to undertake, the student will get better advice by presenting several alternative analyses to the advisor or committee than by bringing in only one. The alternatives also act as a catalyst for bringing out fresh ideas as the student discusses the area of proposed investigation.

THE TOPIC ANALYSIS FORM

The topic analysis is essentially a simplified proposal form, providing a rough outline of factors relating to a dissertation. The parts are as follows:
1. Problem, hypothesis, or question
2. Importance of research (why it is worthy of doctoral research)
3. Theory base for research
4. Significant prior research
5. Possible research approach or methodology
6. Potential outcomes of research and importance of each

Figure 8-1 is an example of a topic analysis. The topic analysis should be quite short—two to four pages should be sufficient in most cases. A short, concise description is needed at this juncture. A few comments about each section may help in preparing this type of analysis.

TOPIC ANALYSIS

Candidate Clark G. Flint   *Date* September 29, 19—

1. Problem, Hypothesis, or Question

Decision models are built to handle risk aversion by the users, but human decision makers are erratic in risk-aversion responses.

Major questions in area are
1. What are the major determinants of variations in risk-aversion behavior by human decision makers?
2. Is relative risk-aversion constant across problem situations?
3. Does experience reduce variations in risk aversion?
4. Can education or simulated experience reduce variations in risk aversion?
The fourth question is the one to be researched.

2. Importance of Research

In the design of decision systems, a decision maker with a given risk aversion is usually assumed. But there is evidence (such as Allen, "Risk Aversion in Production Scheduling," *Journal of Business Research*, July 1994, pp. 475–490) that the decision models are less effective than one would hope because of variations in patterns of risk aversion. There is, therefore, a need to evaluate methods for reducing variations in risk aversion by a decision maker. Burnham states, "There is an urgent need to understand the risk aversion phenomenon and to find and evaluate mechanisms for altering risk-aversion behavior if the new decision systems are to be effective."

3. Theory Base for Research

The research will be based on two components of personality theory: risk aversion and risk taking. Personality theory suggests each individual has propensities that place them on a scale between high risk aversion and high risk taking. The differences are based on childhood experiences. Personality theory also suggests risk-aversion propensities can be altered by training experiences. Tested, theory-based instruments are available for measuring risk aversion.

4. Significant Prior Research

There are a number of studies of risk aversion as determined by personality and environment. Hurst ("Constancy of Risk Aversion," *Journal of Decision Psychology*, January 1995, pp. 120–131) experimented with ten college students and concluded that absolute risk aversion was affected by the problem, but the relative risk aversion evidenced by different subjects was not changed. Wadell ("Effect of Trauma on Risk Aversion," *Journal of Decision Psychology*, February 1990, pp. 5–14) ran experiments that suggest traumatic experience is effective in changing risk aversion for broad classes of related phenomena. No reported research has been found on the effect of education and simulated experience on reducing variations in risk aversion.

5. Possible Research Approach or Methodology

Five methodologies for research are possible. One or more may be used. One through three are proposed.

1. Use a group of students and measure variations in risk-aversion behavior prior to taking the decision sciences course in the fall semester, immediately following the course in December, and six months after taking the course in May.
2. Use a group of inventory controllers taking a course in scientific inventory management. Measurement before, after, and six months after.
3. Use a group of students and measure the change in variability of risk aversion after using the inventory management decision simulator, which provides experience in handling uncertainty by means of decision rules.
4. Use a group of inventory controllers and measure change after use of inventory management decision simulator.
5. Observe changes in card playing behavior (Poker and Hearts) by students who have received instruction in assessing the probability of certain combinations of cards.

Instruments: An instrument to measure risk-aversion variation will have to be constructed and validated. Perhaps it can be constructed from parts of existing personality tests, such as the Alison battery and the Jann test for objectivity.

The inventory management decision simulator is available. A data generator to produce the desired stimuli will need to be added.

8-1. cont'd.

6. Potential Outcomes of Research and Importance of Each

Outcomes are contributions in part of cases; others probably not.

1. Immediate Effect of Education

	Students	Controllers
Variability Reduced	Contribution	Contribution
Variability Increased	?	?
No effect	No contribution	No contribution

2. Six-Month Effect of Education. Same as 1.

3. Effect of Simulated Experience

	Students Only
Variability Reduced	Contribution
Variability Increased	?
No effect	No contribution

The increase in variability is difficult to interpret and is not as strong a contribution as reduction in variability, unless a theoretical basis for the result can be found.

8-1. cont'd. Topic analysis form (all references, and so on, are hypothetical).

Problem, hypothesis, or question. This states what the dissertation will deal with. If hypotheses are appropriate, they should be stated. If the type of topic is not amenable to statement as a hypothesis, then the problem or question should be clearly stated.

Importance of the research. This addresses the question of whether or not the research is important or significant enough to justify doing. If there is some statement by an authority as to need for this research or if it can be demonstrated that this research is significant to a major activity, then this or related reasons should be concisely stated in a short paragraph. The importance of a dissertation need not be earthshaking, but no dissertation should deal with a trivial or inconsequential topic.

Theory base for research. This part of the topic analysis identifies tentative generalizations, concepts, or frameworks from past research that provide the rationale for the research to be performed. A problem or hypothesis does not suddenly emerge; there is some theory basis for believing the problem has a solution or the hypothesis is sound.

Significant prior research. This part mentions the major preceding research. It need not be exhaustive when topics are being selected, but the student should make a quick investigation, taking perhaps 10 to 20 hours, to look at the major research work on the topic.

Possible research approach or methodology. This section of the topic analysis is extremely important because it outlines how the student proposes to approach the research. Is it via questionnaire, observation, simulation, data collection, measurement, or algorithm solution? The approach should be explained as precisely as possible but may still be in a very rough form. Alternative methodology should be included. Most doctoral candidates have taken a research methodology course that has described alternative methodologies.

Potential outcomes of research and importance of each. The contents of this section are vital to an assessment of the dissertation proposal. For each research approach, the different but possible outcomes should be described. For example, a topic analysis might propose a project to collect evidence by a questionnaire. The questionnaire results would be analyzed statistically to determine if there is a positive correlation between perceived behavior and the responses to questions. The potential outcomes might be

1. a significant positive correlation demonstrating the relationship;
2. a significant negative correlation demonstrating the reverse of what was expected;
3. a lack of correlation (probably proving nothing);
4. an inability to obtain satisfactory responses on the questionnaire.

In this particular case, perhaps only one of the potential outcomes might be expected to result in an acceptable dissertation. But it may be possible to structure the data collection and analysis so that a negative correlation might also turn out to be acceptable.

The objective of the topic analysis is to assist the candidate in eliciting helpful comments and alternative suggestions. Therefore, if there are viable alternatives, these should be included (or prepared as a separate topic). Note in the sample shown in Figure 8-1 that several alternatives are suggested, and one is indicated as being preferable.

SELECTING AMONG THE ALTERNATIVE TOPICS

Some topics can be eliminated from further consideration because time or cost are too great. The dissertation advisor and committee may reject other topics as unsuitable. One topic may turn out to be far superior and end the selection process. However, if there are several topics to choose among, the selection should proceed by assessing for each topic the following two probabilities:

1. *The probability of successful completion.* To assist in this assessment, make two lists for each topic.
   a. A list of the expected chapters in the dissertation
   b. A list of major activities required to do the dissertation together with time estimates for each
   If it is difficult or impossible to outline the dissertation and the steps to complete it, this indicates potential difficulty

in completion. Many students want to do too much. A student may propose to perform a simulation, build a prototype, and perform an experiment, when one of the activities is sufficient. It is important to assess the difficulty of carrying out such activities. If it cannot be planned, it probably cannot be done.

2. *The probability of acceptance of the completed research as a dissertation.* This consists of two sets of probabilities.

   a. The probability that each of the outcomes will make a contribution to knowledge

   b. The probability that the committee will accept each of the results as a contribution

There are, of course, other factors such as personal preference, personal standards of research quality, the dissertation as a basis for future work, professional development, and funding.

The final decision is a personal one, but a student should be aware of the relative risks of various topics. A candidate may still choose a risky topic over a "safe" topic, but the choice should be made with an awareness of the risk.

The Proposal

The idea of the topic analysis is to make it short so that it is feasible to prepare several for alternative topics. When one of these topics is finally chosen, the dissertation proposal should be prepared. It is an expansion of the topic analysis and will be used as a work plan for the dissertation. Whereas a topic analysis of 2 to 4 pages is adequate, a complete final proposal might contain 10 to 30 pages. Many students make proposals too lengthy. The literature review is often included. Because it may be quite long, it is appropriate to include it as an appendix to the proposal.

The structure of the proposal (with some idea of reasonable page length) is approximately as follows:

	Section of Proposal	Reasonable Page Length
1.	Summary	1–2
2.	Hypothesis, problem, or question	1–3
3.	Importance of topic	1–2
4.	Theory base for the research	1–5
5.	Prior research on topic	1–7
6.	Research approach or research methodology	2–8
7.	Limitations and key assumptions	1–2
8.	Contributions to knowledge (for each potential outcome, if there is more than one)	1–3
9.	Descriptions of proposed chapters in dissertation	2–3

The *summary* section of the proposal contains one or two paragraphs summarizing what the dissertation project is to do and how it is to do it. The *hypothesis, problem, or question* section is similar to the same section in the topic analysis but is amplified and refined. The same holds true for the section on the *importance of the topic*. The *theory base for the research* section expands the section in the topic analysis.

The *prior research* section should be expanded over that which was included in the topic analysis. It should be more comprehensive because there should now be a search of all major sources of information. If there has been considerable prior work, it can be summarized. This section might consist of from one to five pages. Too many pages indicates a need for summarization, because this is the proposal, not the dissertation itself. Alternatively, it may be an appendix to the proposal.

The *research approach or research methodology* section should be as explicit as possible. The data collection, experiment, or observation method should be explained. If a questionnaire is to be used, for example, the questionnaire methodology should be explained, and perhaps examples of the major types of questions to be asked should be mentioned. Population and selection or sampling procedures should be outlined. If a simulation is to be used, the major elements of the simulation should be defined. If an experimental situation is to be used to collect data, there should be a description covering the subjects, the apparatus to be used, procedures to be followed, data to be collected, and the instruments to be used in data collection. Observation subjects, sites, and frequency should be explained. Obviously, there are many unanswered questions. The idea is to sketch the research approach as clearly as possible. Major questions yet to be decided should be listed.

The *limitations or key assumptions* section is important because it defines the limits of the dissertation work. It is common for students to try to do too much, and the limitations and key assumptions section is useful in defining how much the student will undertake, and in describing key assumptions to govern the building of the model, conducting of the experiment, or observing. This should be explicit—"The research will not ...."

The *contributions* section is similar to the section in the topic analysis and can be written in more detail.

The *chapter descriptions* further define the dissertation. Each chapter can be described in terms of its major headings or by a short paragraph describing what will be covered in that chapter. It should be as specific as possible, but because this is a proposal document, the chapter descriptions should be brief and highlight the structure, rather than give much detail. Most dissertations follow a standard format consisting of the following chapters or sections:

1. *The introduction.* The general problem area, the specific problem, why the topic is important, research approach of the dissertation, limitations and key assumptions, and contribution to be made by the research are described.

2. *A description of what has been done in the past.* This is a complete survey of prior research. If prior research is limited, this description might be combined with Chapter 1; if there is extensive prior research, the results might have

to be divided into two or more chapters. The prior research review is normally an important section of the dissertation because the description of what has been done provides background to the research. It also documents the fact that the candidate's research is unique because the work of the dissertation has not been covered by prior research.

3. *A description of the research methodology.* One or more chapters may be used to describe the research method. For example, the chapter(s) might describe a simulation, a data collection technique, a measurement technique, an experiment, observation, concept development method, or a historical method of analysis. In essence, this section describes how the research was conducted.

4. *The research results.* The results of the chosen methodology are reported; the data are presented, the conceptual framework is described, the historical analysis is defined, the observations are categorized, or the comparative studies are explained.

5. *Analysis of the results.* This may be included with prior chapters depending upon the type of dissertation. This is a key section because it explains the conclusions or understanding that can be drawn from the data and the implications of a theory.

6. *Summary and conclusions.* The dissertation is summarized with emphasis upon the results obtained and the contribution made by these results. Suggestions for further research are also outlined.

With the general structure of a dissertation plus the characteristics of the specific dissertation in mind, the student is usually able to define the chapters of the dissertation. The chapter descriptions can be useful in helping to focus on the objective of a completed, accepted dissertation.

The preceding list of chapters defines a typical dissertation. An alternative format used in a relatively small percentage of dissertations is an essay format. The main body of the dissertation consists of a few (about two to four) essay chapters. There are two reasons for this format. The first is that the content of the dissertation consists of two or more topics that can be presented as separate essays. For example, a dissertation to model family dynamics might consist of three models (each an essay chapter), one for parent to parent dynamics, a second for parents with children, and a third for children to children. The second reason for the essay format is that the essay chapters can be designed as separate articles for journal publication. If the content of the dissertation lends itself to the essay format and the advisor and committee are supportive, this format may be used; otherwise, a more traditional format is probably advisable.

The proposal is a plan for the student to follow. It also provides the dissertation committee with information by which they can approve or reject the project. Approval does not mean automatic approval of the dissertation. But if the proposal is explicit, the committee approval implies that when the proposed work is properly done and clearly documented in a dissertation, there is a high probability that the dissertation will be accepted. A well-done proposal, when accepted by the committee, forms a type of contract (in a personal rather than a legal sense) between the candidate and the committee.

Refining a Proposal

The first proposal is not usually the final proposal. There is a process of refining in which reviews, critical comments, and suggestions are incorporated into revised drafts, which are reviewed. The end result of the review and rewriting (and perhaps starting over with a new proposal) is a complete, crisply defined proposal.

The process of moving from an idea for a dissertation to a concise, well-defined proposal is sometimes the most difficult task of the entire dissertation. It is not unusual for candidates to take six, eight, ten, or more months to define a topic. There is no simple recipe for approaching the process, but some hints may prove helpful.

NARROWING THE SCOPE

The point needs to be repeated—almost every student starts with a project that is too large. One way to narrow the dissertation topic is to attempt to subdivide it into more than one dissertation. Each subdivision is analyzed as a topic. The result may be to choose only one of the subdivisions, and this will usually prove to be a smaller, more manageable topic. For example, a student who wished to study the writing of doctoral dissertations might start out with the topic: "An Investigation of the Factors Affecting Completion of High-Quality Doctoral Dissertations and a Proposed Method for Improving Performance." This can be subdivided into at least three topics, for example, the following:

1. An investigation into individual productivity differences and the time taken to complete dissertations
2. An investigation into the factors affecting the quality of a doctoral dissertation
3. An investigation into a systematic method for managing a doctoral dissertation with some results from a pilot application.

Note that by separating out three dissertations, the scope of each is much better defined and much more likely to be completed.

The student might also consider what the research is trying to accomplish—that is, the anticipated result. If this is difficult to define, a useful technique is to imagine that the dissertation is complete and the final chapter with summary and conclusions is being written. What will be the conclusions? What might be the main points of the results? By trying to draft the conclusions, the main thrust of the dissertation should become clearer and this will help to narrow the scope.

CLARIFYING THE PURPOSE OF THE RESEARCH

Students should try to avoid a "fishing" approach to research. A student who collects much data and then applies multiple regression techniques to see what comes out is not likely to be able to differentiate between spurious and real correlation or to have collected all relevant data. This example is perhaps obvious, but students who collect data or begin interviews without a clear idea of objectives are likely to commit the same fault.

One of the best ways to define the objectives of the research is to state hypotheses that the research methodology will accept or reject. For example, the first of the previous examples of dissertation topics might be stated as a hypothesis that "time taken by candidates to complete doctoral dissertations is a function of: (list)." By listing the factors, the data collection methodology and analysis procedures can be related to the factors that are thought to be important. It is sometimes useful to introduce a competing theory, rather than only defining null hypotheses based on a single theory.

Some topics are not amenable to hypotheses statements. For example, conceptual development and comparative analysis are not usually amenable to hypothesis statements. The third example of a topic was the investigation of a systematic dissertation management method and pilot study. Because this topic is difficult to state as a hypothesis, the research methodology can be clarified and defined by restating the topic in terms of a set of objectives for the research, such as the following:

1. To develop a useful approach for the use of doctoral candidates (approach will be synthesized from management theory and psychological theory)
2. To support the validity of the approach by reference to research and theory in management and psychology
3. To demonstrate feasibility of approach in a pilot study
4. To provide support (but not statistical evidence) for utility of approach by a pilot study

THE DISSERTATION PROPOSAL • 95

Note the fact that the student plans to build an approach (a model of the dissertation completion process) using accepted theory from other fields. Experimental and other evidence from these fields that have been reported in the literature will be used to support the fact that the conceptual structure is sound. The pilot study is useful (although not always necessary) in demonstrating the feasibility of the approach. A small pilot study may also provide data suggesting the utility of the approach, but the sample is usually too small to be statistically significant.

CHECKING FEASIBILITY OF RESEARCH METHODOLOGY

Despite the advice to delay data collection until a proposal is prepared, there are some cases where some preliminary investigation is desirable to check the feasibility of research. Some examples will illustrate such situations.

Case 1: The proposed dissertation research methodology is highly dependent on the use of a panel of experts. There should be some discussion with one or more experts during topic formulation in order to get some insight into the practicality of the technique and the probability of obtaining usable data.

Case 2: The proposed methodology involves the initiation of a prototype instructional program in the school. The success of the dissertation depends on a school's willingness to have a prototype program and the availability of persons to carry it out. There should be some preliminary investigation during the proposal writing stage to assess the probability of these conditions being satisfied for the research.

Case 3: The proposed methodology into the time taken for doctoral dissertations requires that a sample of recent doctorates and a sample of "all but dissertation" candidates, at varying stages of completion, be surveyed.

This depends on locating the current address of these subjects. A preliminary investigation of the quality and availability of the university address files is important in assessing the feasibility of the methodology. A pretest of a proposed questionnaire might provide evidence on both the questionnaire and the address file.

The cases illustrate that there are times when some preliminary investigation is required to get sufficient insight on the problem, the methodology, or the state of the data in order to be able to make a good proposal. In these cases, it is wise to draft the clearest proposal possible before conducting the investigations. After these investigations, revise the proposal. A first draft proposal will serve as a guide to the preliminary investigations.

EVALUATING FEASIBILITY VIA A SCENARIO

One method for testing feasibility is to write a short scenario, or outline, of the actions, activities, and responses that can be expected as the dissertation research proceeds through the crucial phases. Such a scenario may reveal some important data collection or analysis steps that are difficult or impossible to perform. If a student cannot visualize a research scenario from the current point through to completion, it is likely that the research topic is not a good one.

PROPOSAL SEMINARS

Proposal seminars (either formal or informal) can subject the proposal to the ideas of a larger group. Such a presentation should be made as soon as a fairly complete proposal is written, instead of waiting until the research work is well in progress. If the faculty have not provided such a review, the doctoral candidates in an area may wish to do this on an informal basis. Students may get so close to a problem that they cannot see it in perspective; a review session with faculty or other students may help to clarify the proposal. It is important that such seminars be supportive and helpful, rather than a mini-exam, so that candidates will seek advice and constructive criticism. At one university, the proposal seminars became so critical of the research that candidates would not present a proposal until they were almost finished with the research. This negates the major benefit that should come from the seminar—to help the student evaluate (and further define) a proposed topic under investigation.

METHODS OF PRESENTING THE PROPOSED RESEARCH

The ways in which the proposed research is presented can often help define the dissertation proposal. Two examples will illustrate the method of presentation as a factor in clarifying the dissertation.

Example 1: Four researchers have done work with a population similar to that being proposed. The dissertation proposal needs to show the relationship of the prior research to the proposed research in order to (1) define both the similarities and the differences, and (2) evaluate the potential contributions of the proposed research. These objectives can be achieved by presenting the past research and proposed research in a research comparison table (Figure 8-2).

Example 2: The proposal has a hypothesis that there will be changes in career development after the introduction of a career exploration unit in a tenth grade English class. The testing of the hypothesis hinges on the operational definition of *career maturity*, as it relates to the particular classroom exercises. The table of expected research effects (Figure 8-3) was prepared to show which scales in a career maturity inventory might be expected to change

CHARACTERISTICS OF RESEARCH DESIGN

Researcher	Population	Sample Size	Experimental Method	Type of Reinforcement	Reinforcement Schedule
Allon & Michael	Hospitalized schizophrenics	19	2 phase: baseline and treatment	Approval and ignoring	Intermittent on 1 to 3 intervals
Allon & Azrin	Hospitalized chronic depressed females	47	3 phase: contingent, noncontingent, and contingent	Tokens awarded to be exchanged for goods	6 experiments, each with a different reinforcement schedule
Atthowe & Krasner	Hospitalized veterans 22 yr. median stay	60	3 phase: baseline, 3 mo. shaping, and 11 mo. treatment	Tokens and social approval	Contingent on behavior specified in advance
Panek	Same as Atthowe & Krasner		Compared common associates learning with token reinforcement and punishment		
Proposal	Day Treatment Center Veterans	73	2 phase: 2 wk. baseline and 8 wk. treatment	Tokens worth 25 cents	Contingent on behavior specified in advance

8-2. An example research comparison table as a method of relating a research proposal to prior research in a field.

Career Maturity Inventory Scale	Effect of Classroom Exercises X = change expected O = no change expected	
	Self-Concept Exploration Topic	Satisfactions and Rewards of Work Topic
Attitude Scale		
a) Involvment in choice process	X	O
b) Orientation toward work	O	X
c) Preference for career choice	X	X
d) Independence in decision making	X	O
e) Conceptions of the choice process	X	X
Competence Test		
a) Knowing yourself	X	O
b) Knowing occupations	O	X
c) Choosing the job	X	X
d) Planning for the job	O	X
e) Having problem-solving ability	X	O

8-3. Examples of expected research effects.

because of the experimental intervention. The "X" indicates where change in scale scores might be expected because of the classroom exercise. The "O" indicates no change is expected.

A CHECKLIST

The following checklist is not exhaustive, but it suggests useful questions a student should ask during a self-appraisal of the proposal.

1. Does the proposal have imagination?
2. Is the problem stated clearly?
   a. Are the hypotheses clear, unambiguous, and testable?
   b. If there are no hypotheses, are the objectives clearly stated? Can they be accomplished?
   c. Is the problem too large in scope?

3. Is the methodology feasible?
   a. Can data be collected?
   b. How will data be analyzed?
   c. Will the analysis allow the acceptance or rejection of the hypothesis?
   d. Is the population to be sampled overused? (Navajos must be tired of anthropologists, and *Fortune*'s 500 companies must be tired of surveys.)
4. What might the results of the analysis look like? (A useful technique in clarifying the proposal is to try to sketch the form of the tables or other results from the data analysis. The axes of graphs can be labeled and the probable shape of curves estimated. The expected results from correlation, factor analysis, or analysis of variance can be sketched.) Ways of presenting observational results or concept development can be shown.
5. What are the consequences to the dissertation if
   a. the experiment fails;
   b. data cannot be obtained (for each major item of data);
   c. only a small amount of data exists;
   d. the analysis is inconclusive;
   e. the hypothesis is rejected or accepted?
6. Can major research activities be listed?
7. Can a time estimate be attached to each major activity?
8. Is the dissertation trying to do too much?
9. If the answer to question 8 is yes, what can be dropped or reduced to make the project of manageable dimensions?
10. If the student will have to complete elsewhere (against good advice, but it does happen), is the dissertation portable—that is, can it be completed away from the university?

CHAPTER 9

The Dissertation Time Schedule and Budget

While the proposal is being refined, the student should also prepare a time budget and time schedule. Students (and professors) tend to underestimate the time required for completing a dissertation. A formal, detailed estimating approach is likely to yield a better estimate than an overall estimate without any breakdown. All of the estimates use work hours or work months (of 175 work hours). These are converted into elapsed time by a separate computation, taking into account the percentage of time a student can work on the dissertation.

Standard Times

There are no standards for how long a dissertation should take. There is evidence of time differences for different subject areas, universities, and advisors. Some estimates were presented in Chapter 2. These will be expanded in this chapter as bases for preparing a time schedule.

Table 9-1 presents the authors' estimates of the expected time required for doctoral dissertations. The basis for standard time is the estimated median time for doing a good dissertation if the student follows a systematic approach to the management of the dissertation project. This estimate underlies many of the other estimates presented in this chapter.

There are a number of variables that affect these estimates.

TABLE 9-1. STANDARD TIMES FOR DISSERTATION

		Range	
	Standard	Low	High
Page length (see Figure 2–1)	225	100	450
Total effective work months from topic formulation to acceptance	15	11	22
Breakdown: (work months)			
Topic refinement and proposal development	2	1	3
Search prior research in depth	1	1	3
Research and analysis activity	7	5	12
Writing, editing, and proofing	5	3	8
Elapsed time taking into account delays (with full-time work on dissertation)			
From topic formulation to acceptance	18	14	30
From approved proposal to acceptance	14	12	25

*Based on estimates by authors.

Some of these are listed; the student must assess how such factors will affect personal estimates of completion.

Variable	*Comments*
Discipline by student (ability to stick to project)	Good self-discipline reduces time.
Quality of dissertation	Standard estimate assumes good quality (say 70 to 85 percentile on a subjective scale of quality). If average quality (50th percentile) is assumed, time *may* be reduced, but this does not always follow.

Articles or papers written	Many students wish to have articles published or papers presented before entering the job market. These can be related to the dissertation research. This activity will extend the time to completion.
Hours devoted per month	Standard hours in a month are 175. Many students spent more than this on the dissertation; others think they do but don't.
Random events	A spouse becomes ill, the house burns down, there are university riots, new software reduces the effort for analysis, and other similar events may occur.
Advisor response time	Can be quite variable for same advisor.
Job interviews and moving to a new job	Often necessary but disruptive.
Predissertation development activities	A student who selects a topic early and follows the development activities outlined in Chapter 5 may be able to reduce the standard elapsed time (but not necessarily the time spent). Many acivities will have been done prior to formally beginning the dissertation in connection with course work, and so on.

The reason for being quite specific in time estimates, even at the risk of error, is that many students have unrealistic ideas of the time required for a dissertation. Most think it will take less time than it does, but every so often a student starts talking about a four-year project. Advisors are naturally reluctant to say how long it takes to do a dissertation for fear of misleading a candidate. These estimates may provide the basis for discussion in doctoral research seminars where candidates who recently completed their dissertation may report their times and comment on the standard times.

Preparing the Time Estimate

There are several ways to approach a time estimate. One method, illustrated in Figure 9-1, requires the student to

1. define the expected dissertation structure (major chapters and sections within chapters as being prepared for the proposal);
2. estimate the page length by chapter;
3. estimate tasks;
4. estimate times by task;
5. estimate elapsed time.

The time estimate form assumes it is being prepared after the topic has been selected and during the refining of the proposal. The following discussion will follow the format of the estimating form in Figure 9-1.

REFINING OF DISSERTATION STRUCTURE

The students are left somewhat on their own for this section, but a few guidelines expressed in work hours may be helpful.

Range in Work Hours	Low	High
Preparation of revised proposal	50	250
Detailed outline of dissertation	10	50

IDENTIFICATION

Student _____ Advisor _____

Date of estimate_____

Title or description of proposed dissertation:

REFINING OF DISSERTATION STRUCTURE

	Student Estimate in Work Hours
Preparation of revised proposal	_____
Detailed outline of dissertation	_____
Other	_____
Total	☐

FURTHER SEARCH OF LITERATURE FOR PRIOR RESEARCH

Sources to be Searched	Est. No. to be Searched	Hours for Each Standard Estimate	Student Estimate	Total Work Hours
Journal articles	_____	1.0	_____	_____
Books	_____	10.0	_____	_____
Dissertations	_____	10.0	_____	_____
Government documents	_____	3.0	_____	_____
Other (documents, computer searches)	_____		_____	_____
		Total		☐

9-1(a).

RESEARCH ACTIVITIES

	Estimated Work Hours
Examining supporting literature (use 5–6 hours per 100 pages)	_____
Preparing instrument for collecting data (questionnaire, simulation, or experiment)	_____
Obtaining agreement of organizations, groups, and/or individuals to participate as subjects	_____
Testing instrument or procedures for collecting data	_____
Collecting data (running experiment, doing questionnaires, observations, etc.)	_____
Analyzing data (including all preparation for analysis)	_____
Developing concepts and theories	_____
Analyzing results	_____
Other	_____
Total	[ ]

WRITING, EDITING, REWRITING, AND PROOFREADING

Chapter	Approximate Title	Est. Pages	Work Hours Per Page Std. Est.	Work Hours Per Page Rev. Est.	Work Hours per Chapter
_____	_____	_____	4	_____	_____
_____	_____	_____	4	_____	_____
_____	_____	_____	4	_____	_____
_____	_____	_____	4	_____	_____
_____	_____	_____	4	_____	_____
_____	_____	_____	4	_____	_____
_____	_____	_____	4	_____	_____
	Summary and conclusions	_____	8	_____	_____
	Bibliography	_____	6	_____	_____
	Appendices	_____	–	_____	_____
	Total				[ ]

9-1(b).

TOTAL ESTIMATED WORK HOURS

Refining of dissertation structure _____

Further search of literature for prior research _____

Research activities _____

Writing, editing, rewriting, and proofreading _____

Total work hours [_____]

ESTIMATED COMPLETION DATE

	Month	Year
Starting date for completion estimate	____	__

Working time in elapsed months

$$\left(\frac{\text{Total estimated work hours}}{175} \right) \left(\frac{1}{\substack{\text{Percent of time} \\ \text{devoted to thesis}}} \right) \quad \text{____}$$

Estimated completion time (no delays) _____

Delays expected:	Months
Data collection delays	_____
Data analysis delays	_____
Chapter reading delays	_____
Final reading delays	_____
Typing and printing delays	
Other delays	_____

Estimated final completion date
(ready for defense) [_____]

9-1(c).
Time estimate for completing doctoral dissertation using chapter and task estimates.

FURTHER SEARCH OF LITERATURE
FOR PRIOR RESEARCH

The literature search estimate here is the one to establish the originality of the research being performed. It takes longer to search a book than an article. Some standard times are shown but the student should apply individualized estimates. The same approach may be used to estimate the literature review time connected with research activities.

RESEARCH ACTIVITIES

Different research activities are listed, but the student should define the main research tasks connected with the dissertation and estimate the time required for each. The total time in work hours will probably fall in the 1,000 to 1,500 work-hour range.

WRITING, EDITING, REWRITING,
AND PROOFREADING

This is an area where students consistently underestimate the time required to document the research. The standard estimate is four hours per double-spaced typewritten page of final manuscript. The student might remember doing a five-page paper in one evening and applies that time estimate, but it is not sufficient. In fact, many students require more than four hours per page. The summary and conclusions usually must be rewritten several times, so the standard time for the final chapter is double, or eight hours per page. The bibliography is time consuming to set up and proofread, so a six-hour-per-page estimate is used. Appendices may include computer printouts, copies of questionnaires, letters used in data collection, and tests used. These still take time to include, but there is no way to establish a standard estimate.

Scheduling Activities

After preparing a gross time budget, the activities should be sequenced through time. This can be somewhat rough but should be complete. Figure 9-2 shows a sample format. This method is commonly termed *Gantt chart*. When using the Gantt chart of activities, major review points should then be planned. This will be important in working with the advisor and the committee. Scheduling software may facilitate Gantt chart preparation, but it is not necessary. Figure 9-3 is a sample format for critical review dates.

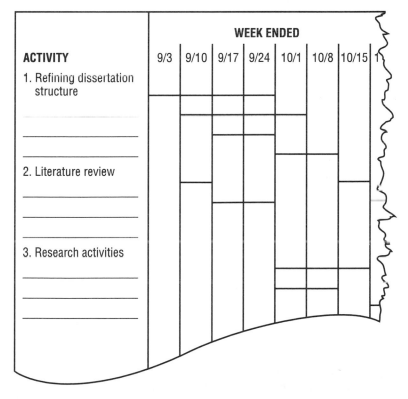

9-2. Scheduling of dissertation activities (Gantt chart).

Candidate _____

CRITICAL REVIEW DATES

Review Activity	Reviewed by	Earliest Date	Latest Date	Planned Date
Review of final proposal	Committee	_____	_____	_____
Review of methodology or approach	Advisor et al.	_____	_____	_____
Review of questionnaire and sampling plan	Committee	_____	_____	_____
Review of test sample results	Advisor	_____	_____	_____
Review of revised sampling	Committe	_____	_____	_____
Review of draft of Chapter 1	Advisor	_____	_____	_____
Review of revised Chapter 1	Committee	_____	_____	_____

9-3. Schedule of critical review dates.

If several activities are linked together so that completion of one depends on the completion of one or more others, they are said to form a "critical path." In this case, the student might wish to make a simple critical path analysis (see literature on critical path, CPM, or PERT such as F. K. Levy, G. L. Thompson, and J. D. Weist, "The ABC's of the Critical Path Method," *Harvard Business Review*, September-October 1963).

Reminder

The important concept is realistic planning and this must depend on realistic time estimates. The best estimates are usually made by breaking down the activities into small tasks and combining these estimates. The standard estimates should provide a check for individual estimates. A student who arrives at a six-month estimate may be fortunate; more likely, a poor estimator. A student should not be dissuaded from making time estimates because there is a particular task that cannot be estimated. Estimate the other activities and then include a pessimistic, optimistic, and best estimate for the hard-to-project activity. It is better to have an imprecise estimate than no estimate at all.

A last point is that different subject fields have different modal times (the most common time students take to complete). If the modal time is 25 months instead of 14, this may reflect requirements in the area, or it may merely reflect dilatory work habits that students in the area have adopted because others before them did it that way.

A Dissertation Budget

Many candidates are surprised at the costs of preparing the dissertation. A researcher may have a grant to cover the direct research costs, but the grant will probably not cover the costs of keying, copying, and binding the dissertation. These costs are small relative to the cost of doing the research, but they may be large relative to available funds at the time of completion. A budget that plans for them will ease the financial demands of the dissertation completion.

A budget is also useful in formulating requests for dissertation support from various funding sources. Without a budget, it is difficult to estimate what support is needed and to select items most likely to be funded.

It is not feasible to make a budget template that will fit all doctoral dissertations. However, once a topic is formulated, it is relatively simple to prepare a budget. The problem is not in the difficulty of doing it; it is in taking the time and effort to do the budget part of the plan. There are significant individual differences in ability to intuitively budget expenditures. Given these large individual differences, the best policy is an explicit budget for the costs involved.

Dividing the costs of doing a dissertation into research, writing, and completion may be useful. Consider some of the following items.

EXPENDITURES FOR RESEARCH

Expenses of experiments (instruments, supplies, incentives, rewards, meals, snacks, software, and so on)
Printing of instruments
Postage
Telephone
Travel to research sites
Copies of dissertations, articles, books, and so forth needed for literature review
Data entry when large volume of data
Computer software for analysis or computer time
Reproduction of materials used in research

EXPENDITURES FOR WRITING

Software for word processing, graphics, and presentations
Key entry of text if not done personally
Reproduction of drafts for committee review
Cost of editing if necessary because of limitations on ability (especially with some students who write in a language other than their native language)

EXPENDITURES FOR COMPLETION

Final document layout and preparation if not done personally
Draft copies for review
Reproduction of copies as required by the university
Binding as required by the university (including copies for committee and others)
Other filing and graduation fees

CHAPTER **10**

Working with an Advisor and a Dissertation Committee

The advisor is a crucial figure in the completion of a dissertation. The university entrusts the advisor with considerable power and responsibility in the dissertation acceptance process. The committee members are also important but less so than the advisor. The advisor and committee are responsible for assisting the candidate; the student, for presenting material in a way that effectively uses the scarce advisor and committee resources. This chapter explores procedures the student can follow to help make interaction with the advisor and committee effective. Problems can arise in these relationships. Students may get so involved in their research problem that they forget that advisors are human beings. The chapter explores typical situations and possible solutions.

Aids to Effective Interaction with an Advisor and a Committee

The student should recognize that there are many demands on the advisor for time and attention, and there frequently are interruptions that keep the advisor from devoting attention to the candidate. The candidate's problem is usually how to improve the probability of a timely and helpful response from the advisor.

The suggested method consists of written notes, outlines, issue summaries, scheduled times for meetings, and meeting agendas. 1. *Provide written notes of meetings.* When meeting with the committee, the candidate should make notes. Immediately after the meeting the candidate should write up these notes, summarizing what was talked about and any conclusions that were reached. The candidate should keep a file of the notes and provide copies of all notes to the advisor and, perhaps, to the committee, if relevant. If there have been a number of quick question-and-answer contacts with the committee, the candidate may wish to summarize the significant ones every two weeks or every month. The rule is that the candidate should take responsibility for documenting the decisions and actions communicated by the advisor and the committee. Two examples of notes are included—one, a note on sampling procedure agreed

---

Candidate: Clark G. Flint   *Date:* November 1,1997

Summary of Sampling Plan Review

A sampling plan review was held with Professor Euwe of the statistics department. Professor Euwe has had prior experience with this type of problem.

Professor Euwe agreed to the general procedure but expressed reservations about the adequacy of a sample size of 100 for discriminating the effects of cultural background. He reserved judgment until the pretest results.

He suggested that the statistics department "Cross Cultural Analysis Program" would provide an appropriate computer analysis of the data.

I have examined the program documentation, and it provides all analysis we have agreed upon except the h index, which I will program separately.

10-1. Note summarizing significant discussion.

Candidate: Clark G. Flint   *Date of Meeting:* Oct. 16,1997

Summary of Meeting with Ph.D. Committee

In attendance: R. G. Smith, Advisor
                  John Hoffmann
                  Gary Gray

Absent: William Jones

1. **Review of Revised Outline of Chapter One**
    The committee expressed agreement with the revised outline. Professor
    Gray asked that the section on cultural background of the problem be
    expanded to include the recent research by Maxwell and Pawlofski.
    This was agreed upon .

2. **Review of Proposed Data Collection Procedure**
    The proposed method of paired samples was approved. After review-
    ing the computations of sample size, the committee suggested that a
    sample size of 100 instead of 150 would be sufficient. The final
    decision will await the results of a pretest of a sample of 10.

3. **Review of Revised Dissertation Schedule**
    The revised schedule, calling for final reading of the complete draft in
    July, was discussed. Professor Hoffmann indicated that a change in
    plans makes a July reading unfeasible, but he will be able to read it
    in the first week of August. The schedule was therefore revised to a
    faculty return of draft manuscript by August 9.

4. **Next Meeting and Other Reviews**
    a. A sampling plan review with Professor Euwe of the statistics
       department has been scheduled for November by the candidate.
    b. A review of the experimental procedures prior to the pretest is
       scheduled with Professor Smith on November 8.
    c. The pretest will be conducted November 12–13. A written report
       of the pretest will be distributed on November 21.
    d. The committee agreed to review the results of the pretest on
       November 28 at 2:00 p.m. in the 6th floor conference room.
       The meeting is planned for about 1 hour.

10-2.   Report of committee meeting.

to by the committee member with the highest competence in the area of sampling (Figure 10-1), and the other, from a formal meeting of a committee (Figure 10-2).

2. *Provide outlines and issue summaries with each batch of materials the committee is asked to read.* A candidate hands an advisor a 50-page manuscript to read with no outline and no indication of what issues are important. It is understandable that the professor puts off getting to it. A better approach is to provide the following set of materials:

a. *A transmittal note.* This lists the materials being given and a gentle reminder of the date by which the advisor or committee has agreed to return comments. (See Figure 10-3.)

b. *Issue summary.* A short statement that tells the contents of the batch of materials and gives a short description of each issue (or area in material) to which the reader should direct attention or for which the candidate would especially like comments. (See Figure 10-4.)

c. *Outline of each chapter.* These outline the major headings. If only one or two chapters are being provided,

---

Candidate: Clark G. Flint   *Date:* January 15,1998

TO: Dissertation Committee: Smith, Hoffmann, Gray, and Jones

Attached is the revised draft of Chapter 2 for your review and comments. The committee agreed upon January 31 as the date for comments to be returned. It would be most helpful to me if I could have your comments by that date. I would appreciate having your comments on some ideas listed on an attached issue summary.

10-3. Transmittal memo.

Candidate: Clark G. Flint   *Date:* January 2,1998

Issue Summary for Chapter 2

This chapter discusses past research on the influence of cultural background on decision-making style. Important issues to be noted in the chapter are:

1. Cultural background is defined. Note that I have not included the Murphy factors for reasons described in the chapter. Do you have comments?

2. The research of O'Neil and Elwin is rejected. Because of its lack of control, the results are considered to be dubious. Do you agree with this rejection?

10-4. Issue summary.

> it is helpful to attach the outline of all chapters, so the reader can keep the material received in context. (See Figure 10-5.)

    d. *The material to be read.* This should always be printed double-spaced. The candidate should keep a control copy and the readers should write notes on their copy.

3. *Schedule meetings.* Plan ahead and schedule the necessary meetings. A schedule for the dissertation work and a schedule of critical reviews (described previously) should assist the candidate and the advisor in deciding on the meetings to schedule. Distribute materials at least a week before (and longer if a large number of pages). Send a separate reminder notice of the meeting. Arrange well in advance for a place to hold the meeting if this is a problem. A good policy is to schedule the next meeting at the conclusion of the current meeting, because there can be a group discussion and resolution of conflicts in schedules.

4. *Provide action agendas for meeting.* The candidate's advisor may act as chairman of the meeting, but the candidate

Chapter 2

**A Review of Past Research on Influence
of Cultural Background on Decision-Making Style**

DEFINITIONS

Decision-Making Style

Cultural Background

RESEARCH INTO DECISION-MAKING STYLE

The Miller-Kontel Study—1938

The Elmoore Study—1961

The Jones Study—1993

The Maxwell and Pawlofski Study—1994

A Synthesis of Findings

*RESEARCH ON INFLUENCE OF CULTURAL
BACKGROUND ON DECISION-MAKING*

10-5. Chapter outline.

should discuss with the advisor whether or not a proposed draft agenda would be useful. Or the student may prefer to be less formal and merely discuss meeting objectives. However, an agenda should still be prepared, either by the student or by the advisor. After the advisor approves the agenda, it should be sent along with the reminder notice to those who are to attend. The agenda should describe each point to be discussed and decisions, if any, to be made (Figure 10-6).

5. *Provide written responses and periodic progress reports.* If a committee member asks a question that the candidate cannot answer immediately but has agreed to provide an answer for later, the answer should be written and sent

(keeping a copy on file). The file of reports, agendas, and questions forms a partial diary of the candidate's activity. A periodic written progress report is useful if the candidate is not meeting regularly with the committee. For example, if a student leaves the university or the professor goes on short-term leave so that there is a lack of personal contact, a regular (monthly or bimonthly) report is desirable. It is frustrating to have an advisee who is supposed to be working on a dissertation but who never reports in. Even a short, half-page summary is better than no report.

Advisor and Committee Problems and Suggested Solutions

Even if a candidate approaches the advisor/committee relationship as described, there can be problems. No one can advise

---

AGENDA

CLARK G. FLINT DISSERTATION MEETING

November 28, 1997

3:15 p.m. in BA 6th Floor Seminar Room

1. Discussion of Chapter 3. Specific points to discuss are

   a. Sampling plan

   b. Questionnaire, especially part II

   c. Review of pretest

   d. Problem of analysis of comments

2. Report of computer program to be used in analysis

10-6. Agenda for meeting of committee.

about these matters in advance, but some ideas may help a candidate if one of these problems occurs.

1. *The advisor goes on leave, goes to another university, takes a nonuniversity position, or dies.* The regulations of the university will govern in each case, but a good dissertation file will assist in making a change if an advisor dies or leaves the university. If the candidate has followed a well-planned and well-documented dissertation strategy, one of the other members of the committee will probably be willing to take over. Or another member of the department may be asked to serve. A more sensitive situation arises when the advisor goes on leave. Often another member of the committee can serve as temporary advisor until the advisor returns. If, however, the advisor is the key person affecting the completion of the dissertation, the candidate may wish to move to the new location as well, provided that the advisor agrees. When counting the cost of such an action, the student must also count the cost of a delay in the dissertation. In most cases, however, the advisor role can be taken over by another. The current advisor should advise as to a replacement. Before a change is made, the student should frankly discuss with both the current advisor and the proposed replacement who the advisor will be in the event the current advisor should return before the dissertation is complete.

Many universities allow faculty members who go to another unversity to continue to act as advisors for candidates in process. Again, the decision to keep the old advisor or to get a new one depends on how critical the advisor is to the success of the dissertation and on the stage of the dissertation. If the dissertation is almost finished, the current advisor should be used; if just begun, a new advisor should probably be sought.

2. *One of the committee goes on leave.* The problem is similar to that of an advisor, except the advisor will assist in making a decision on committee replacement.

3. *The advisor or committee members will not read the drafts.* A common complaint by students is that faculty will not read prepared drafts. But many students make it difficult. Contrast the following two approaches and consider which is most likely to yield results.

Typical: Student suddenly appears with drafts. No chapter outlines or issue lists. Professor feels as if the draft will require hours of concentrated time to read and comment. It is difficult to find such a large block of time.

Better: Student has provided advance notice of material to be read, and committee have agreed on dates for return of material. Chapters have outlines and issue lists, so that the professor may segment the task of review.

In the case of an advisor who does not read the drafts, it is sometimes useful to try to get a commitment as to a date when the draft will be read and request scheduling a meeting of the committee to discuss the drafts. If this is not an appropriate strategy, the most tactful thing to do is to ask for the best estimate of completion and return on that date. Keep repeating the process. Meanwhile, keep working. A well-defined dissertation will allow such parallel development.

If a committee member delays excessively in reading a draft, the advisor may assist. If there is an outline and an issue summary, the student may suggest a verbal discussion with the committee member of the points on the issue list.

4. *The advisor becomes intransigent or obstructionistic.* Fortunately, it doesn't happen often. In most cases, it is probably best for the student to meet privately with the advisor and express concerns. One should state feelings, but not accuse. It promotes better, freer discussion to say "I feel that you no longer think I can complete the dissertation." The advisor may be reacting negatively to some of the student's behavior. The student may have been discourteous or there may have been an honest difference about the research. If the discussion does not resolve the issue, the student can wait a little to see if things work out. If the problem continues, the student should explore whether or not the advisor wishes to continue. If the professor does not, the student should select a new advisor; if the professor does, the student must try to work it out again. A student may get some help from others on the committee or other faculty, but this is generally the last resort, rather than the first action.

5. *One of the committee becomes intransigent or obstructionistic.* The advisor is usually the key, but first a talk with the committee person, expressing fears and asking if there is something that should be changed, may be in order. It is generally easier to change committee members than an advisor, but it is far better to have the member request the change (on the basis of workload, change in interest for dissertation) than for a change to be forced.

11

Management of Dissertation Activities

Prior chapters have described how to select an advisor and committee, select a topic, prepare a proposal, and work with an advisor and committee. This chapter will describe the management of the individual dissertation activities. Emphasis will be on the management of activities that are general to most dissertations. The chapter will, therefore, not cover specific methodology considerations.

Research Records

The dissertation is a major project extending over a considerable period of time, so accurate and complete records need to be maintained. A student may not see the need to record an idea or something read in a journal, thinking—"I will remember it"—but the result is that many good ideas are lost, and many journal citations have to be found again. Some suggestions on research records are an investigator's journal and a coding and filing system.

THE INVESTIGATOR'S JOURNAL

The candidate should keep a diary or journal of research investigations. This can be a loose-leaf notebook, but the bound type of journal, commonly used by scientific investigators, might be more serviceable. Notes should be made of work performed, of decisions made, and of suggestions made by the advisor or committee members. These notes and suggestions will form the basis for some of the written communications with the advisor and the committee described in the previous chapter. However, if any questions arise about the summaries, the original notes are contained in the investigator's journal. The investigator's journal thus forms a chronological diary and record of work that has been performed and ideas, suggestions, and comments that are important to the dissertation.

A CODING AND FILING SYSTEM

Almost immediately, the candidate will be faced with the task of coding and filing information that accumulates. A logical system for coding and filing is by using major subtopics within the dissertation. For example, if the dissertation consists of six chapters and there are, within these chapters, 20 major subtitles, each of these subtitles can be the basis for classification of references, ideas, and other information as data is collected. A separate section of a notebook, a file folder, or computer file may be used for each of these sections. Each idea, quotation, or data analysis is coded according to the section under which it falls. Usually it is a wise idea to have a general section for each chapter for the coding of information that does not seem to come under any of the subtopics but is relevant to the chapter as a whole. The information collected should clearly be labeled as to source and the date it was obtained. A reference date is especially important for information obtained from personal interviews. Journal references should be complete.

It is wise for the student to decide immediately on a bibliographic and reference style. The exact style is not important. It is more significant to decide on a single style. Many universities specify a style manual or specify one of several style manuals as acceptable. Three examples of commonly used style manuals are

- *A Manual for Writers of Term Papers, Theses, and Dissertations,* Kate L. Turabian. 6th ed., rev. by John Grossman and Alice Ben. Chicago: University of Chicago Press, 1996. Designed for research papers and dissertations.
- *Publication Manual of the American Psychological Association,* 4th ed. Washington, D.C.: The American Psychological Association, 1994. One of the major style manuals for North America. Used by many social science disciplines.
- *MLA Handbook for Writers of Research Papers,* 4th ed., Joseph Gibaldi. New York: Modern Language Association of America, 1995. Includes a detailed index and many examples. Covers nonprint media, CD-ROMs, electronic texts, and E-mail.

Select one of the style manuals and follow the reference format. Putting all bibliographic references in the selected standard format will ensure that all necessary bibliographic reference information is obtained. Also it will not be necessary to rearrange or redo the references when dissertation drafts are written. Many word processing software packages even provide formatting assistance for common reference styles.

One copy of each draft prepared should be maintained in both a paper and a computer file. As early drafts are revised, rewritten, and changed, it is sometimes useful to be able to return to the original, which was the basis for the revision. The file represents a chronological record of the progress of the dissertation effort. There is one other important reason for having such a file. It is possible to lose drafts of dissertation chapters—briefcases are lost, or the mail does not get through. Whenever a university building burns there is always the story of professor X or student Y whose entire work of several years has been destroyed in the fire. Therefore, a candidate should always preserve one copy of each written draft, preferably in a place separate from the rest of the records. Then, in the case of fire or any other disaster, the entire work is not lost. This happens infrequently, but the cost of a backup file is not substantial, and the peace of mind is probably worth the cost. The chronological file, if stored in a separate location, can be the backup file.

Planning and Control of Daily Work

One of the principles for doing work such as a dissertation is to provide structure for the work. Because structured work generally takes precedence over unstructured work, the management task is to put enough structure into the dissertation activity that it assumes a priority over other less important activities. Some suggestions are to begin each week with a planning hour and establish tasks for the week, estimating times for each of the tasks. A larger number of tasks than can actually be completed should be outlined, putting priority on their completion. The extra tasks function as alternatives; candidates can begin these tasks if the planned task cannot be completed for some reason. At the next planning session, the actual times can be compared with the estimated times, and decisions can be made as to effectiveness of work and the amount of time to be allowed for activities in the coming week.

Writing the Dissertation Drafts

Writing activity is somewhat personal, but certain approaches seem to be successful. The student should decide upon a format for chapter headings, subheadings, and further subdivisions. These are usually included in a manual of style. The exact format is not nearly as important as selecting a pattern and following it consistently.

The chapter or subchapter to be written should be outlined in detail before writing begins. An outline function in a word processor may be useful. This will result in much more coherent and cohesive writing. Sections should be drafted as soon as possible. Dissertation writing should be viewed as an iterative process, and a chapter, consisting of four subsections, may be written a section at a time, as the material for each of the subsections has been obtained. This will result in a somewhat choppy chapter, but the editing activity is usually much less difficult than the original composition. References should be included in the original draft in a proper form.

A first draft will need to be edited and refined. One approach that works quite well is to read an entire chapter or major subsection and then decide if the organization appears to be acceptable. If so, the chapter is edited for individual sentence structure, style, and content. If not, a new outline is prepared, and the chapter is reorganized. Then it is edited to smooth out the roughness that comes from reorganization.

Obtaining Methodological Assistance

Many candidates need assistance with such matters as statistical analysis, computer processing, or questionnaire design. It is always useful to have a member of the committee who will assist in reviewing the candidate's plans. Some universities provide special groups to assist doctoral candidates and others in such matters as statistics and computer processing. Candidates may also find other students who have special competence and who are willing to help if the amount of assistance required is reasonable.

There are a number of computer packages to do statistical processing. Most universities have consultants who will assist in the use of the statistical packages, and the candidate should seek their advice—that is, in such a way that the probability of getting correct advice is high. Many candidates go to the software consultant and mumble something about needing some statistical analysis done. A likely response might be "There's a manual at the bookstore." Such advice is not very helpful. The student should prepare for seeking processing advice by preparing a description of the problem, the data that are available, the form of the data, the amount and the type of analysis required. In utilizing computer processing, the candidate should make sure the program being used correctly does what is desired. User documentation should be read carefully. Particular attention should be paid to controls, which will assure the student that all of the data has been processed in the intended way. For example, the program should provide a count of the number of records being used by the program.

Many candidates design their questionnaires and data collection forms without regard for the problems of data entry for computer processing. This may present substantial difficulties and introduce errors. A candidate who does not have prior experience should examine the process of data entry prior to completing the questionnaire or data collection design. The candidate should always take steps to control the quality of the input data and the quality of data entry. At a minimum, a listing of input data should be examined and tested for errors.

A candidate should be able to explain the method of determining that the results of the computer analysis were correct. Results can be tested to check if they are reasonable, or a problem can be run in more than one way, to provide a cross-check of the results. Computer statistical packages that are commonly used are correct, but they will not work properly with incorrect specifications or incorrect data. The candidate should carefully evaluate the correctness of the specifications for processing and results.

Coping with Problems

A dissertation that is planned to be written over a period of one and one-half or more years will never be done without the occurrence of some problems. One area of concern is personal, physical, and mental health and relationships; the other area relates to coping with failure situations.

PERSONAL HEALTH AND FAMILY RELATIONSHIPS

Doing a dissertation can be a terrible grind, and there is considerable pressure on candidates to work long hours. However, this can lead to poor health and exhaustion so that the candidate is not alert enough to do a good job. A work pattern should be established, based on a plan of work for each week. However, there should also be times for recreation. This is especially important should there be a wife, husband, or children involved. Many students mention the strain that the dissertation causes regarding spouse and family. However, one of the most difficult problems, apparently, is not that the candidate is working long hours but that the spouse and family feel that there is no time that belongs to them. Advice that seems to have been quite successful suggests that the candidate should block out certain times during the week for family activities. For example, the candidate who has children may identify one evening, from 5 to 8 p.m., for family activities with the children. The candidate might agree with the spouse that Friday and Saturday nights are available for social activities with friends and that part or all of Sunday will be kept free for activities appropriate to their situation. Such a plan not only improves the mental and physical health of the candidate, but it is likely to keep spouse and family relationships more healthy.

THE BEST LAID PLANS, OR COPING WITH FAILURE SITUATIONS

This manual has been written from the view that a planned systematic approach to the dissertation will assist a candidate in avoiding most of the pitfalls and difficulties encountered in completing the dissertation. Our experience is that even well-planned projects sometimes go awry. This happens for many reasons, some of which are beyond the control of the candidate. We have attempted to identify some of these below with some suggestions for coping with them.

1. *The project does not go as planned.* Research leads one into unknown areas. Even when one is familiar with existing research and related literature, and when one attempts to anticipate the problems and difficulties in collecting data, judgments can be in error or new directions can become more fruitful. When this happens, it is important to reconsider prior decisions to see at which point(s) the research needs to be redirected. For example, one student had developed a carefully designed study of the effects of a communications training program. The plan was to test the program in the field. After several months of planning, checking detail, and doing a pilot run, a block was encountered in persuading actual clients to consent to participate in the research. A strong incentive was needed or it would be necessary to move the research back into the laboratory. Because there were no funds available for incentive, the decision was made to make a "laboratory test" and offering the communications training program free in exchange for the research data. Fortunately, the data being collected were sufficiently different from those previously collected so that it was worthwhile to complete the research.

2. *Momentum is lost.* The graduate experience makes many demands. A student is often married, has family obligations, works part-time, and attempts to maintain a normal social life. With all of this, the dissertation can be easily set aside and let go for a period. When this happens, the data get rusty, procedures are interrupted, or the writing becomes stale. Then it is especially difficult to get back to the task. Perhaps the most important remedy in such cases is a good dose of honesty. Advisors are in a difficult position, not wanting to take over responsibility for the success of the project, yet not wanting the student to fail. Most wait patiently, gently prod and encourage, but must rely on the student's initiative to become active

again. If the student can confront this responsibility and admit the need for extra help in getting started, the advisor can usually work out a plan for systematic follow-up until the student has assumed full responsibility again.

3. *Discouragement and depression.* Doctoral students are *people*. They are subject to the same range of emotions, fears, and joys that others experience. Students sometimes get discouraged or depressed, and that interrupts progress on the dissertation. There are good reasons for this. As we have emphasized, the project is a large one requiring from one to two years to complete. The candidate is usually working alone. The data are often complex and sometimes confusing. The process can become downright drudgery at times, particularly during the analysis and writing stages. What was to be a creative contribution to the field turns out to be, at certain times, routine, hard work. Because of lack of experience and accurate information the student may feel alone, overwhelmed, and incompetent to complete the work. As the data are collected the student may fear that the results will not confirm the hypotheses. In general, there is little positive reinforcement to keep the project moving. It is quite natural for depression to set in if these periods are not realistically anticipated and planned for.

Acknowledging these possibilities often allows a candidate to plan activities that are personally rewarding and, thus, fend off discouragement. It is particularly important to build a support group of other students and some faculty with whom the process can be shared, including the bad days as well as those moments of discovery. Good advisors recognize the probability of such times from their own down periods doing research and will spend time with advisees helping them overcome their discouragement.

Central to success is the partnership between a student and an advisor. Each has an important, even critical, role to play. If a student can accept that and, as a true partner, share both success and failure experiences with the advisor, most of the troublesome times can be overcome without serious loss of time.

4. *Writer's block.* A student may find it almost impossible to write. There may be psychological reasons for this. For example, a student may be insecure about the results and avoid writing chapters in order to avoid exposing this imagined failure, or there may be difficulty in knowing where to start. Most writers, including professors, have experienced writer's block. The most successful approach is to start writing, even if some of the pages must be discarded. However, it probably does not work well to start with chapter one of the dissertation and write in linear fashion; rather, write sections of chapters as work is being done. For example, write the explanation of the literature search and the research-and-analysis procedures as these are formulated and performed. Write notes for various chapters, including the first and last chapters. Start formulating tentative interpretations. The reason chapter one is often left to the end is that it introduces and defines the entire dissertation. Notes for the last chapter can be written as ideas and interpretations emerge, but the final draft of that chapter will be one of the last things written.

5. *Someone else publishes the same research the student is doing.* This raises a fundamental issue of dissertation contribution to knowledge. The issue must be resolved with the advisor and dissertation committee. Duplication of work is rarely a problem in the social sciences. Two people who work on the same topic, but employ different methodology, can generally both claim a contribution. However, it may present some problems. The student should examine carefully what the other researcher has done and note differences in purpose, scope, and methodology. Look for the unanswered questions that the other

researcher has not explored. Generally, with a little extra work, the student can add to and extend what has been done. Probably only one-fourth to one-fifth of the total dissertation time is connected with the key "contribution" factors, so even a complete duplication, requiring restructuring of the contribution elements, is not the same as starting over. The danger of such duplication is reduced by timely completion. It is the person who spends five years on a dissertation who is generally caught by duplication

6. *The dissertation is rejected.* If the committee decision or the final oral result in a rejection of the dissertation, what then? If the student has been following a suitable schedule of reviews, it is unlikely the committee will reject the dissertation, rather they are likely to suggest modifications. The candidate should respond to the requests, and the dissertation will generally be accepted. It is useful to get criticisms that are expressed in terms of what needs to be done. Professorial courtesy will generally allow committee members to suggest minor modifications without objection from other members. But if such suggestion(s) will present a real problem, it is appropriate for the student to ask if the suggested work is necessary for the acceptance of the dissertation. Commonly, committee members make suggestions not only for revision of the dissertation but also for future work on the topic after acceptance of the dissertation. A suggestion involving considerable research will probably fit into the future work category.

CHAPTER 12

The Defense and Publishing the Results

As the student nears the end of the dissertation writing, there are two matters to plan for. These are the defense of the dissertation and one or more journal articles reporting the results of the research.

Preparation for the Defense of the Dissertation

Requirements vary from university to university, but a common requirement is that the student defend the doctoral dissertation before a committee probably consisting of the advisor, the rest of the committee that has assisted in the dissertation, and two or more outside readers who have not been involved in supervising the dissertation.

If the student has done a good job of writing the first chapter, which explains why the dissertation topic is important, and has done a good job of writing the final chapter, which includes a description of the contribution made by the dissertation, then the task of defending the dissertation will be much easier than if that format is not followed. The examining committee is likely to ask questions such as the following:

- Why did you use that research methodology?
- Why did you analyze the data that way?

- Why didn't you analyze the data differently (for example, by using a specified technique commonly used)?
- It was an obvious extension to do . . . why didn't you do it . . .?

After being so close to the dissertation topic and doing so much writing and editing, the student may have lost sight of the overall flow of the dissertation. In preparation for the defense, it is often helpful to prepare an outline, which can be a short presentation, perhaps 15 minutes, describing why the problem was important, how it arose, what others have done, the methodology that was followed, the results of the investigation, and the contribution to knowledge from the dissertation. In essence, this is an after-the-fact dissertation proposal format. The student is going back to the questions that needed to be answered before the dissertation was begun. The questions are the same, but the answers can now be precise. The dissertation is complete, so the student should be able to clearly explain the reasons for limitations of scope and for exclusions, such as not undertaking parts of the problem or doing certain types of analysis. Some common reasons for limitations and exclusions follow:

- It would have been too time consuming, and the committee advisor agreed that it would be sufficient to do the analysis performed.
- The extension might be interesting, but it was not included in order to keep the dissertation within reasonable scope.
- Preliminary investigations showed the technique was not feasible.

The student should not hesitate to explain the contribution made by the dissertation, but should not try to claim more for it than is really there.

The defense of the dissertation may bring out various suggestions. Then the student must decide whether or not more work should be done or if the dissertation should be changed to reflect the suggestions. Generally, the candidate can rely on the advisor and other committee members to help put suggestions in perspective and to decide what suggestions should be implemented. The following are some examples of suggestions that might come up in the defense session and reasonable responses a candidate might make:

Suggestions or Comments	*Possible Responses*
1. I think you should apply the analysis to the problem and see what results you get.	a. I will be able to do that, because it does not take much time. I will then present the results to my advisor and the dissertation committee. If you feel it is advisable, I will be happy to include the results in the dissertation.
	b. I think that I can do it, but I would prefer not to hold up the dissertation unless you feel that it is necessary for approval. I will, however, do the analysis and, if it is interesting, will include the results in the journal article that I am writing to report the research.
	c. The analysis sounds interesting, but because of the possible time required to do it and the uncertain results, I would like to handle it as a postdissertation activity.

2. I have the following edi-
torial comments:

a. You state the case too
strongly on page 139.

    a. If the committee is agree-
able, I will make the corrections you suggest and
will present them to my
advisor for approval before
the dissertation is sent for
final binding.

b. You draw an invalid
conclusion from the
quotation by Nevert.

    b. I tend to disagree with your
comment about the conclu-
sions I have drawn because
. . . . I can indicate the alternative view that is taken
by others, if that would
improve the dissertation.

The candidate should be willing to respond in a positive way
to small suggestions, but if suggestions seem to involve a good
deal of work, it is advisable to get the committee to discuss
them fully and arrive at a consensus as to what should be done.
The candidate should probably summarize, at the end of the
dissertation defense, any additions or corrections the committee
has requested be made, dividing them into those that must be
incorporated in the dissertation before it is finally approved and
those comments that involve suggestions that are better handled
by future work or future research.

The Journal Article

If the dissertation is a good one, it generally deserves to have
the results reported in a scholarly journal. So many students are
worn out by the time they complete the dissertation that they
never complete the journal article. Only about 15 percent of the
American doctoral dissertations have been reported in a journal

article.[1] In order to improve the probability of a journal article from the dissertation, a student should plan for it during the dissertation process. At the time the dissertation is receiving the final reading, there is generally a delay period, which the student can profitably use for preparing the journal article. The student should not think that all that is needed is a copy of the dissertation, a pair of scissors, and a couple of hours to produce a journal article. The journal article needs to be condensed and the style needs to be slightly different from that of the dissertation. Therefore, the student should allocate perhaps 40 to 80 hours to the preparation of the journal article.

When writing the journal article, one approaches it in the same way as writing the dissertation chapter. A detailed outline is prepared to ensure that the flow of ideas is correct. The article is written, edited, rewritten, reedited, and rewritten until an acceptable draft is prepared. An appropriate journal is selected, and the article is sent to the editor in charge of such articles. The student and advisor may wish to have one article prepared for a scholarly journal in the field, but the student may also wish to do a more popular type of article for a journal or magazine having wide readership.

A question that arises is the extent to which the advisor or another member of the committee should be invited to participate in the journal article. In general, courtesy dictates that the advisor should be invited to participate in the journal article. Most advisors have contributed substantially to the quality of a good dissertation and, therefore, they deserve to be asked about being coauthor, even though many prefer to let the student do it alone. The ordering of the names in such an article is really not too important. The fact that it is a doctoral dissertation report makes the relationship of the authors quite clear.

---

[1]Julie L. Moore, "Bibliographic Control of American Doctoral Dissertation," *Special Libraries* (June 1972): 289.

The Book

In recent years, less than one percent of doctoral dissertations have been published as books.[2] One reason is that many dissertation topics are not suitable as books; another reason is that a dissertation must be rewritten to be publishable as a book. In order to be viable as a regular commercial venture, a book should generally have a well-defined market and a potential five-year sale of several thousand copies. However, a book need not be published by a commercial publisher; there are specialized markets, such as university presses and professional organizations that publish monograph series. These will publish books written for a smaller, more specialized audience.

If you feel your dissertation subject matter is suitable as a text, keep in mind the need for rewriting. A dissertation generally has a fairly rigid structure and uses a scholarly, "academic" prose. A book needs to flow more easily. The dissertation generally has a cautious, formal style with footnotes documenting every significant statement; the book needs a more readable, confident style, dropping many footnotes. The following are suggestions for revising or rewriting to produce a book:[3]

1. Reduce or eliminate the review of the literature. A summary or background discussion is more suitable in establishing a place for your work.
2. Reduce the number of levels of subdivisions. Use the flow of the text to make the separation of ideas.
3. Reduce repetition. In many cases, the introduction, analysis, and summary chapters of dissertations have much overlapping material because the style of dissertation chapters tends to be repetitious.

---

[2]For a description of the differences between a dissertation and a book written from it, *see* Frances G. Halpenny, "The Thesis and the Book," *Press Notes*, (University of Toronto Press, January 1968).

[3]*See also* David Horne, "Six for Jaffe," *Scholarly Books in America*, VII, no. 4 (April 1965): 2.

4. Eliminate all footnotes that do not add substance. Footnotes that merely support reasonable assertions can usually be dropped.
5. Rewrite for readability. Short, straightforward sentences without jargon are needed. Read it aloud to identify sentences that need rewriting.

Conclusion

This small book has traced the successful path of the dissertation from the time it was a suggestion, reflection, or a beginning idea, to its presentation to the professional public in a journal article. It has examined ways to take those interesting ideas and formulate them into researchable hypotheses or problems. The testing of the hypotheses and investigation of important problems have become manageable by planning and systematically approaching what would have been, otherwise, a nebulous and, at times, seemingly impossible task.

The essence of the approach in this book is the partnership of candidate and advisor; the initiative for planning, preparing, searching, and testing must lie with the candidate, while the responsibility for supporting, encouraging, critically evaluating, and suggesting lies with the advisor and the committee. When this partnership is strengthened by the systematic use of the suggestions and approaches offered here, the task can be not only manageable but quite enjoyable.

Using Computer Software for Productivity in Dissertation Activities

Computer software is perhaps the most important tool for improving productivity in dissertation activities. Computer software may be used in such activities as

- searching for prior research or other relevant information;
- doing research such as experiments or modeling;
- storing and retrieving data;
- analyzing data;
- writing the dissertation;
- editing the dissertation.

Before describing the use of software for these six types of activities, the selection of software and the productive use of software will be described.

Selection of Software for Dissertation Activities

There are specialized software packages used in different academic fields for common research activities. A student will generally be familiar with these packages. The discussion will focus on the generalized software packages used generally across all disciplines.

The rate of introduction of new software products or new versions of existing software is so rapid that any description of specific software would be quickly obsolete. However, the basic functionality that provides productivity in knowledge work such as dissertation activities is more fundamental. A useful approach to finding and using software in a dissertation is to focus on the activities of the dissertation that are likely to benefit from computer software functions. Having identified the functions needed, look for software that has them. For example, the following functions are contained in software packages:

Function	*Software Packages*
Search for data	Communications software including Internet and World Wide Web access
Model processes	Flowcharting, drawing, and process-modeling software. Financial-modeling software. Simulation software
Plan and schedule	Spreadsheet software, personal information management software, or project management software
File and retrieve data	Database software
Author	Word processing, including spell checker, grammar checker, and outliner
Analyze data	Spreadsheet software, statistical software, and specialized analysis software
Present results	Presentation software, including graphics, charting, and multimedia

A single software package may provide more than one function. For example, a spreadsheet package can be used for simple financial modeling, analysis, simple presentations, and simple database management involving only one table. Complex financial modeling may benefit from a specialized financial modeling package, superior presentation graphics from a specialized presentation package, and databases with more than one table from a specialized database package. In other words, the selection and use of specialized software packages may depend on the need for their greater capabilities.

Productive Use of Computer Software

The financial cost of computer software is generally small; there is usually a more significant cost to learn the use of the software so that it is productive. The cost to acquire and learn software may be thought of as an investment. The payback comes from savings in performing activities in less time and with fewer errors than doing it manually (or with a different software package). Savings are highest if the software is learned well enough that the clerical activities of use become automatic. For example, a word processor provides the most productivity if the user can concentrate attention on writing while automatically performing the different setup, formatting, and keying functions.

Because there is an up-front investment in a software package and the payback is in a stream of benefits over its use, a doctoral student may not see the benefit and, thus, not invest in software that will improve productivity. In the student's mind, the investment is not justified by the immediate demands of a day or a week. The reverse may be true. A student may be so captivated by new software that there is overinvestment and productivity is lost.

Software is most productive if it is applied in the same way for the same type of problems. The setup of documents, charts, analyses, and presentations generally takes more time than the writing. Productivity is improved by reuse of templates, layouts, formats, and so on. Software supports this kind of reuse. Setting up a standard template of headings, titles, and subdivisions for a dissertation chapter is an up-front investment. It reduces overall time because the template can be used for all chapters. Setting up a standard way to label charts provides similar reuse benefits. Standard layouts, formats, and templates can be saved and reused.

Software for Searching for Prior Research or Other Relevant Information

Software is a necessity in searching for prior research. The following are examples of ways to search using software:

- Search the World Wide Web. The information on the Web is extensive and rapidly growing. The search may turn up leads to published literature and databases.
- Search government and other databases available on-line. Many government agencies have on-line databases. For example, the Securities and Exchange Commission make the reports submitted by companies with publicly traded stock available on-line.
- Search databases of on-line database service providers. A large number of databases are available on-line from providers who charge a fee for access. The fees are generally within the budget of a dissertation if the searches are planned carefully.
- Search the library collections, your own and others. Many databases available on-line for a fee are available through the university library, either on-line or on CD-ROM.
- Search library databases on CD-ROMs. The CD-ROMs are not as up-to-date as the on-line databases but are lower cost for historical searches. Desired references and text can be copied from the CD-ROM for use in the dissertation (properly referenced, of course).
- Search conference proceedings on CD-ROMs. Major conferences in many fields are now available on CD-ROM along with full-text search tools.

The availability of computer search tools allows much more extensive searches than were possible with manual search tools. The disadvantage is that a researcher may be overwhelmed by search results that are not relevant. A useful research skill is searching so that relevant data items are obtained and irrelevant items are reduced. This is accomplished by a search strategy and careful use of search mechanisms.

Searches can focus on specialized databases or broad domains such as the World Wide Web.[1] A Web search strategy will be defined, because this is the most difficult. The principles can be applied to a more narrowly defined domain. Search tools for searches on the Internet range from broad to specialized. Searches on the Web employ tools called search engines. These differ in the way they categorize available information and search for it. Some categorize Web sites into a treelike hierarchy; others read and index sites based on words in the documents at the sites. There are specialized search engines for people and companies. Therefore, a student should learn about several search engines and experiment with them.

Searches may turn up a large number of references. However, many search engines apply a relevance algorithm to rank the references as to likely relevance. This allows the searcher to read the ones most likely to be relevant first. Although the searcher can take advantage of the search engine features, a search strategy should also be employed.

1. Define information being sought. Express it in different ways. Identify different words that might be used (a thesaurus may be useful).

2. Choose an appropriate search engine. Different search engines may provide different results depending on whether the type of information is web sites, topics, software, persons, companies, or Usenet news.

---

[1] Based on a 1996 unpublished course paper by Doug Maltby.

3. Evaluate the number of "hits." If too many, perhaps the search needs to be more specific; if too few, the search may be too specific. Usually the problem is that the search is too broad and needs to be narrowed.

4. Narrow the search. Boolean operations are used to narrow searches. The operators are AND when both terms must be present for a "hit" or OR (often implied) when either can be present. NOT eliminates hits that contain certain undesirable or irrelevant terms. NEAR and ADJ or + or similar terms are used to define the need for terms to be near to one another or directly adjacent. Although AND, OR, and NOT are almost standard, a researcher may need to check on the rules for each major search engine. To illustrate the effect of narrowing the search, a Web search for Abigail OR Adams indicated there were 28,188 instances of Abigail and 360,348 instances of Adams but only 524 of Abigail+Adams and 90 for Adams+Abigail.

5. Validate the information. Examine the results to see if they are based on verifiable facts or opinions of verifiable experts.

6. Apply stopping rules. By following a good search strategy, most relevant information can be found in a reasonable amount of time (reasonable is defined by the nature of the search and the difficulty of finding relevant information). Spending more time may yield some additional sources but the cost is likely to be higher than the value of the added information. Stopping rules may be based on number of valid references, amount of time spent, or added yield from additional efforts.

The concept of a search strategy and stopping rules applies also to specialized databases. Many of these contain only journals within a certain field or topic area. The search engines are usually based on words in the articles. This means that queries may need to narrow the search from general terms often repeated to terms with specific modifiers or terms that are not modified in a certain way.

An important part of the search process for dissertations involving data collection or experimental procedures is a search for validated instruments. These are often reported in the literature along with information on how to obtain them, so a literature search may find them. There are articles that summarize and comment on instruments. Some fields maintain lists on Web pages or in monographs of instruments. A search of Web pages may find instruments that the authors will make available.

Software for Doing Experiments or Modeling

Software can be used to create an experimental environment or collect data when a task is being done on computers. For example, stimuli may be presented via a computer screen and responses elicited from the keyboard or a mouse. If the subjects are doing tasks with the computer, software may be employed to record their keystrokes or mouse strokes.

Software can be used to create financial models and examine the financial results from altering different variables in different combinations. System dynamic models can be created with specialized software to examine the behavior of systems such as economies, ecologies, and population under different assumptions. Queuing models can be written with specialized software to examine effects of variables such as service times on queue lengths and waiting times. These methods can employ existing software. Only in specialized cases is it necessary to write new software.

Storing and Retrieving Data

A researcher will often need to store data for later retrieval. The data may need to be manipulated, such as selecting, combining, and sorting in different ways. Collections of data are termed *files* or *databases*. Although differences can be identified for the two terms, file and database will be used synonymously. A file or a table in a database is based on an object of interest (an entity) about which data items are collected. The set of data items for each instance is termed a record or entity instance. A relational database, the most commonly supported, contains tables related through record keys that are common. A file that contains only one type of record (a flat file) and a database with only one table achieve the same result. A database may have more than one table, adding power to storage and retrieval.

If the data to be stored and retrieved can be expressed as single records in a flat file, a number of software packages can store, retrieve, and sort the records. A word processor can store flat file records with data items kept separate by tabs, commas, or other separators. A spreadsheet processor can store a flat file with each record as a row and the different items in spreadsheet columns. The spreadsheet is superior to the word processor because it uses columns, and columns are easier to manipulate and move. Spreadsheets tend to have input functions that create an input form to ease the task of data input and reduce the error rate. Analysis packages such as statistical software often have database capabilities that may be sufficient.

If there are related tables, the use of a database package is indicated. Even with one table for a flat file, the database package provides some advantages in the use of input forms with validation criteria and ability to do some added functions.

If data is to be collected, stored, and manipulated, a student should consider the data storage and manipulation alternatives and whether an investment in learning to use specialized database software is justified compared to use of spreadsheet, statistical package, or other software file capabilities.

Software for Doing Data Analysis

Software for standard descriptive statistics and other simple data analysis is available as part of spreadsheet packages. However, specialized packages for statistical analysis and other analytical procedures are more likely to have the features and functionality required for dissertation data analysis. Different fields within universities tend to favor different packages. All packages have the main statistics and analytical procedures; they differ on specialized or lesser-used features. Many universities provide assistance with analysis, and they may favor one package over others. A few commonly used statistical packages illustrate the availability of excellent software for data screening and descriptive statistics, regression analysis, variance analysis, estimation and hypothesis testing, and other analysis and processing: SAS (Statistical Analysis System), SPSS (Statistical Package for the Social Science), and BMDP (Bio-Medical Data Package). It is not difficult to move from one major package to another, but the principle of reuse and automatic processing for clerical procedures associated with a package mean that any change from one package to another has some cost.

In some cases, the analysis to be performed is not available in one of the packages. An alternative is to use mathematical and statistical subroutines. These usually require the researcher to write a few statements in a high-level procedural language such as FORTRAN. These subroutines are usually available from the computing center. Subroutines should only be used if a package does not do the analysis desired because the extra effort to learn FORTRAN, although minimal, adds effort and increases the opportunity for errors.

Doctoral students should have experience and reasonable ability to use a major software package for analysis. They should also be familiar with specialized packages for any unusual or seldom performed procedures.

Software for Writing the Dissertation

Word processing has changed the writing of a dissertation. Doctoral students have probably already developed an ability to enter text from a keyboard. Although it is a clerical activity, the ability to do "touch typing" adds to productivity. Touch typing means the entering of text is automatic processing and attention may be directed to formulating and editing the text being entered. If current practice is "hunt and peck," the investment to learn touch typing may yield benefits not only in the dissertation but in a career. There are software packages to tutor a person in entering data with the "touch" method. The same concept applies to entering numeric data. Most computer keyboards have a ten-key numeric pad for data entry. If there will be significant data entry, the doctoral student may increase overall productivity by learning to do touch entry, rather than looking at the keyboard.

A dissertation has a style. Each heading starting with the chapter title is differentiated. There is a style for legends on figures and tables. The style determines the way references are presented and footnotes or endnotes used. The placement of page numbers and the use of headers and footers are determined by the style as are margins, font selection, and font size. The style may be specified by the university for dissertations or may be left to the student.

A student may start writing with the idea that style decisions can be made later. This causes much rework and lost productivity. Making the style decisions when writing begins will allow a style sheet to be specified for the document so that the word processor will assist with the style, will allow the use of the style to become automatic, and will eliminate style confusion.

It is useful to examine various preferences and options with the word processor. Some of these have productivity implications. The following illustrate the kinds of preferences/options and their productivity effects:

- *Default for document folder.* When there is an Open command, the default directory or document folder will be displayed. When working on a dissertation, this is the dissertation folder with dissertation chapters and notes. This eliminates a search for the dissertation folder/directory.

- *Keyboard.* The normal keyboard is usually specified, but if the dissertation involves use of other languages, the keyboard can be tailored with certain keys used for foreign language characters. Example: If Swedish city names are to be written, three keys may be assigned to the special Swedish characters of ä, å, and ö. This eliminates the need to look them up during keying.
- *Quick correct function.* This is a function that corrects commonly misspelled words as they are being keyed. Teh is changed to the. The software builds a table of common errors and correct replacements. The table can be edited to eliminate corrections not wanted. The table can also be used to enter common phrases when a code is keyed. For example, the phrase "management information systems" can be equated with a three letter code "mis." When mis is entered, the software automatically corrects it to "management information systems." A few words or phrases that will be used frequently can be added to the table. Also, difficult words or foreign words can be added. For example, rather than doing the extra steps to enter foreign characters, the foreign spelling can be added to the table as a correction for the spelling using English characters. For example, the Swedish city of Umeå can be entered as Umea and corrected automatically. Each use of this feature gives a small saving, but frequent use can result in significant savings.
- *Recorded macros.* When a sequence of actions is repeated often, it may be recorded as a macro. The sequence is invoked by playing the macro, either by a menu selection or by placing the macro on an icon or associating it with a keystroke.

There are functions that require coding in the document. The most obvious is coding of headings and subheadings for a table of contents. They can be coded as a last step, but it is much better to code them as part of a style. When the dissertation chapters are complete, a generate-table-of-contents function creates a table of contents with page numbers for each level of heading that was coded. This is not only efficient for one table of contents, but because changes in the dissertation will change the pagination and the table of contents, it makes a revised table of contents simple to create.

References and bibliography entries should be entered when the reference is cited. The entry should follow the chosen style and be complete in all respects. The references can be rearranged in alphabetical order by cutting and pasting, but a more efficient approach is to use the word processing package sort commands. If each bibliographic reference is separated by a blank line, the command to sort by first word of paragraph will sort the bibliographic entries by the first word (last name of first author). The sort will not be perfect if there are duplicate last names but it will require little fixing. The sort can be repeated as bibliographic entries are added. The features of the sort can be used to hold some bibliography references until decisions are made to include them or not. They can be placed at the beginning of the bibliography by adding a numeric digit in front of the name. When a decision is made to include, remove the numeric digit and resort. Those excluded are easily removed. The idea is to avoid rework and let the software do tasks such as sorting.

Most word processors provide for automatic backup of work being performed. In other words, every n minutes (n specified by the user), the software copies the contents of the document being written to a computer file. If the computer loses power, the work in progress can be recovered. This backup is useful only until the document is closed. It is prudent to store the work in a file. The store command should be given frequently, usually at each interruption. In addition to frequent save commands, files should be backed up to another medium. The simplest is to back up to a diskette, but alternatives are to back up to a local network server or to a backup tape device. The backup copy should be stored in a safe place, preferably at a location different from the computer being used, in case there is a fire or other disaster.

Software for Editing the Dissertation

The software can assist in eliminating certain types of errors. Spelling errors should be eliminated. Search features should be used to find and examine word uses that may be awkward or even incorrect. Grammar checkers can be useful in identifying poor usage. A thesaurus may be used to find alternate words that are clearer or provide variety. Printing specifications can be used to control for output layout errors.

Spelling errors can be eliminated by use of a spell checker. Quick correction allows spelling errors to be corrected for common mistakes. If the spell checker indicates a word is misspelled but does not have a correction, it means the word is not in the vocabulary of the spell checker. It can be added. This will detect misspelling of the word when it is used later. Uncommon words that are frequently used should be added to the speller vocabulary. This can include place names and proper names. A spell checker will not detect misuse of a word that is spelled correctly. If *too* is meant and *to* is entered, the error will not be detected. Spell checking is effective and has a low cost. It should always be used.

A student will frequently use a few awkward or incorrect expressions. Software may be used to examine each usage to decide if it is correct or should be changed. For example, a student may use *which* instead of *that*. All uses of which may be examined and those not correct can be easily changed. There may be an overuse of a phrase or word. Searching may be used to find and replace some of the uses. There are also instances of incorrect spelling of names or titles. For example, Arthur Andersen (a firm) may be spelled Arthur Anderson. The search function may be used to locate the instances and correct them. Generally, it is risky to make automatic changes (Anderson to

Andersen) because there may be unintended changes as well.

Grammar-checking software may be useful, and are usually included with word processors. Most grammar checkers allow the user to specify the type of document. They are not automatic. The user must examine each item marked and evaluate the suggestion. Perhaps one-third or fewer suggestions are accepted; however, those accepted are often useful. Grammar checkers can detect errors such as mismatch between subject and verb, use of awkward language, use of unnecessary words, and similar errors. But the mechanical nature of the analysis also gives poor suggestions that should be rejected.

A thesaurus is usually included with word processors. It can be used during writing to find a suitable terms or examine alternative terms. In editing, the thesaurus can be used to find alternative words to avoid repeating the same term. Where a term doesn't quite convey the meaning intended, the thesaurus can suggest alternatives. For example, a sentence may have been written with the phrase *angry observors*. If angry doesn't convey the exact meaning, the thesaurus will suggest synonyms. In running this example, 38 synonyms were suggested for *angry*, including *acrimonious, antagonistic, enraged,* and *offended*.

When a dissertation is ready to be printed for review or for binding, there are certain difficulties or errors in output that should be checked carefully. For example, a figure or table should generally follow the reference to it, a heading or first sentence of a paragraph should not usually be at the end of a page (widow) or the last line of a paragraph at the beginning of a page (orphan). Some text should remain together on a page. A new chapter should begin on an odd-numbered (right-hand) page. Specifications made in the word-processing documents will implement these rules. Even after the specifications, a final examination of the output will usually be required to correct output anomalies. In general, it is a good idea to avoid coding end-of-page (making hard pages) except in the last editing, because other changes may make them incorrect.